THE CHINESE
BOOK OF
TABLE TENNIS

THE CHINESE BOOK OF TABLE TENNIS

EDITED AND
WRITTEN BY   Ding Shu De

Wang Lian Fang

Zhu Qing Zuo

Yuan Hai Lu

TRANSLATED BY   Anna Wang

Wang Hui-Ming

DRAWINGS BY   Alison Potter

NEW YORK   1981   *Atheneum*

Library of Congress Cataloging in Publication Data

Main entry under title:
The Chinese book of table tennis.
    1. Table tennis. 2. Table tennis—China.
I. Ting, Shu-te.
GV1005.C473   1981   796.34'6   80-65996
ISBN 0-689-11082-0

Published simultaneously in Canada by McClelland and
    Stewart Ltd.
Composition by American–Stratford Graphic Services,
    Brattleboro, Vermont
Manufactured by Fairfield Graphics, Fairfield, Pennsylvania
Designed by Kathleen Carey
First American Edition

8/81 — Scribner #18645

CHAIRMAN MAO SAID:

"Promote physical education movements.
Improve people's physical condition."

"Develop our capabilities: Do
calisthenics, play ball games, jog,
run, climb mountains, swim, do Tai-chi-
chuan and all kinds of physical fitness
exercises."

CONTENTS

PREFACE

UNDER THE GUIDELINES OF CHAIRMAN MAO'S PROLE-
tarian cultural revolution, physical education in China
has undergone a great and memorable change. Chairman Mao's beliefs penetrated so deeply into the hearts
of the people that cadres and young people hurried
to participate in sports, following his slogan: "Promote
physical education movements. Improve people's physical condition." This revolutionary spirit in physical
education not only improved the physical condition
of the people and enriched their life outside of work,
but also noticeably advanced the goals of the revolution, increasing production and generating higher
work efficiency.

To meet the needs of young people wishing to enlarge the scope of their athletic activities, we are publishing a series of books on physical education, following the Marxist-Leninist concept and Chairman Mao's thoughts. Sports covered in this series are track, swimming, martial arts, weight lifting, ball games, racket games and physical conditioning. Each book offers a brief introduction to the sport as well as an insight into the advanced techniques and training. We sincerely hope that young people will use these books not only to improve their physical conditioning and sports skills but at the same time to learn how others have devoted themselves to the ideals of a socialistic country.

We gratefully acknowledge the author's who are contributing to this series and welcome criticisms and opinions from all readers.

Editors
Young People's Physical Education Series
The Shanghai People's Publishers

THE CHINESE
BOOK OF
TABLE TENNIS

A BRIEF
INTRODUCTION TO
TABLE TENNIS
IN CHINA

PING-PONG* WAS INTRODUCED TO CHINA FROM Europe in 1916. But before Liberation, ping-pong was played only by the privileged and governing class of bureaucrats. The masses of common and poverty-stricken people could not even afford to play the game recreationally, let alone in tournaments. For this reason, ping-pong was not promoted nor developed as a national sport. The standards of technique and strat-

* In China, table tennis is onomatopoetically called "ping-pong." If you say ping-pong a few times with your eyes closed, you will realize how appropriately, poetically and musically the name describes the game. You can almost hear ping-pong being played. In this chapter, we retain the flavor by calling table tennis "ping-pong."

egy were low, and no national competitions were held. Matches were played only locally in big cities such as Shanghai, Tientsin, Canton and Nanking.

After Liberation, under the leadership of Chairman Mao and the Central Government, physical education and fitness programs were initiated. For the first time, soldiers, farmers, workers and young athletes began participating in sports. Competitions stimulated interest and elevated the standards of sports across the country. Our ping-pong champions began to participate in international tournaments and to win acclaim around the world.

In 1953, in Romania, our ping-pong team officially entered the International Table Tennis Championships for the first time. Our men's team placed tenth in Division I and our women's team placed third in Division II.

In the next few years, our teams continued improving their techniques and strategy. They soon reached the summit in play and won many championships. In 1959, at the 25th International Table Tennis Championships, both our men's and women's teams took third place in Division I, and a representative of China won the men's singles championship. Socialistic China has continued to win world recognition for achievements in table tennis.

In April, 1961, the International Table Tennis Championships were held in our capital, Peking. The Chinese team, fortified by sound training and the strategic guidance of its coaches, made a near-sweep of the major titles. A list of achievements follows:

First place: men's team, men's singles, women's singles.

Second place: women's team, men's singles, women's doubles, mixed doubles.

As the ideology of the proletarian revolution continued to stimulate ping pong in China, our players piled up numerous world championships. They took four first-place titles at the 31st International Table Tennis Championships, three first-places at the 32nd championships, and both the men's team title and the women's team title at the 33rd championships.

At other tournaments in the 1970s that drew international fields, players from China were also highly successful. They won the men's and women's titles at the 21st Yugoslavian International Championships, plus the men's singles and the women's doubles, in November of 1975.

That same month, China sent a team of newly trained young players, all born after the Cultural Revolution, to the 18th Scandinavian International Championships, largely with the limited expectation that these youngsters would get experience against international competitors. The results, however, were surprisingly productive. The Chinese players won five titles—men's team, women's team, men's singles, women's doubles and mixed doubles.

The following January, at the Romanian International Championships, the Chinese team took six first-places—the two team titles, the two singles titles, the men's doubles and the mixed doubles.

That was followed in February of 1976 by six

more first places at the Welsh Championships—men's team, men's and women's singles, men's and women's doubles and mixed doubles.

The scene shifted to Shanghai in September of 1976 for the International Friendship Invitational Tournament, at which Chinese players swept the top four places in men's and women's singles, adding the women's team title and second place in the men's team competition.

At the Third Asian–African–Latin American Friendship Invitational Tournament in October of 1976 at Mexico City, 53 countries were represented and China won the men's and women's singles and team championships.

At all of the international tournaments, the Chinese team faithfully adhered to our slogan: "Friendship first, competition second." It was this spirit that made every tournament a success for China, diplomatically gaining friends everywhere.

The secret of how our players achieved such steady worldwide success is that the coaches and athletes all followed the leadership of Chairman Mao in pursuing the teachings of Marx-Lenin-Mao as fundamental in training and strategy.

It is not surprising that, through this revolution in thinking, our athletes attained excellence at these tournaments. Rigid training in the techniques of attack and defense, in maneuvering the ball, in body conditioning through daily exercise and in mental stability with the goal of serving the country, all contributed to cultivating confidence in our representa-

tives. And since the 26th International Championships, the distinctive achievements of our players
have brought a new look to the world of table tennis.

It is of the utmost importance that young athletes
in their growing years develop their bodies through
daily exercise. At the same time, they should be aware
of their moral responsibilities and use their knowledge
and capabilities to continue to improve the standards
of sports.

THE EVOLUTION OF TECHNIQUE IN INTERNATIONAL TABLE TENNIS

FROM 1926 (WHEN THE FIRST INTERNATIONAL CHAM-
pionships were held) to 1950, table tennis players
from Europe won almost all the titles. In fact, out of
117 championships contested in 7 divisions, 109 were
won by European players in that span.

The accepted technique of the period was the safe,
defensive chop. However, after 1950, with the advent
of sponge rackets which enabled a player to impart
strong spins and produce devastating kill shots, table
tennis players gave up the defensive tradition and
started to attack.

Using sponge rackets, the Japanese stunned the
world of table tennis with their heavy spins and
merciless, smashing style. By countering the conven-

tional European defensive tactics with their attacking play, the Japanese won all five men's team championships and four of the five men's singles championships between the 21st and 25th world tournaments.

At the 26th, 27th, 28th, 31st and 33rd International Championships (China did not participate in the 29th and 30th championships) we used a new tactic called the "close-to-the-table-fast-attack." This technique gave China the men's team title five times and the men's singles title four times. In the women's categories, the results generally followed the same trend as the men's.

Then the Europeans converted to the "close-to-the-table-fast-attack" and the Japanese style based on the "loopspin." The combination of the two techniques, blended with the traditional European defensive play, gave the Europeans a share of the major championships between 1954 and 1971.

At the 31st International Championships, Stellan Bengtsson of Sweden won the men's singles title, while Istvan Jonyer and Tibor Klamper of Hungary took the men's doubles. In 1973, at the 32nd International Championships, Sweden won the men's team and men's doubles titles. And in 1975, Hungary won the men's doubles.

Both Stellan Bengtsson and Kjell Johansson of Sweden demonstrated remarkable proficiency in the "fast-hit-attack" and "loopspin" techniques. So did Jonyer and Yugoslavia's Anton Stipancic and Dragulin Surbek. The European players also improved their serves markedly. Surbek, for instance, utilized four or five different serves, which enabled him to win points immediately and attack his opponents effectively.

Tactically, the Europeans employed three basic maneuvers:

1. Fast-hit attacking combined with some loopspins
2. Loopspins combined with some fast-hit shots
3. Traditional chop

Let's examine the elements of the three strategies:

1. *Fast-hit attacking combined with loopspins.* From a central position about one and a half feet from the edge of the table, the advantage is that the player can use either the forehand or backhand attack and is in position to push or block any shots by the opponent. After serving or receiving, usually the player hits a loopspin and follows with attack shots. Under attack, the player can defend with backhand loopspins to forestall the crisis until regaining position to launch a counterattack. Johansson and Bengtsson, the two Swedish players, were masters of this strategy. And so were their Swedish teammates on the women's side, among them Ann Christin Hellman, a strong left-hander.

2. *Loopspins combined with fast-hit attacking.* Standing centrally behind the table, the player is also in position to execute fast and heavy loopspins. There are two offshoots to this tactic. One is mainly to employ forehand loopspins, interspersed with a few backhand loopspins, culminating in a final forceful attack. Stipancic, the Yugoslavian, was an exponent of this style. The other technique calls for forehand loop-

spins and sidespins, interspersed with backhand loop-spins. That was the forte of Stipancic's teammate Sur-bek. Aside from the Yugoslavians, the West Germans and the French also adopted this tactic productively at the 33rd International Championships.

3. *Traditional chop*. The chop was for years the normal European defensive tactic. The theory of the stroke is to upset the equilibrium of the opponent who uses topspin and ultimately gain control of the table to launch a counterattack. With or without a spin, the chop is the best defense against loops. At the 32nd International Championships, the men's team from Hungary and the women's team from Romania were both effective employing this technique.

When the sponge rubber racket was introduced in the 1950s, the Japanese became dominant interna-tionally. They continued to refine their tactics in the 1960s, concentrating on the backhand attack. Most of them were vertical racket holders. Each specialized in one or two tactics. Some of the more accomplished Japanese players of that era and their characteristics of play were as follows:

Nobuhiko Hasegawa: traditional attack technique combined with loopspins
Kohno: fast-hit attacker
Eno: exponent of powerful loopspins
Norio Takashima: chopper
Furukawa: chopper
Tasaka: attacker while standing sideways

At the 33rd International Championships, Kohno and Takashima led a sweep by the Japanese team of the first four places in the men's singles. And at the Third Asian–African–Latin American Friendship Invitational Tournament, in Mexico City, the Japanese won the men's and women's doubles and the mixed doubles.

The women's team from the Republic of Korea is also worth watching. The Korean style and strategy, particularly the foot movement, are most impressive. Poh Ying Shun of Korea was the women's singles winner at the 33rd International Championships, and the Koreans took the women's team and doubles titles at the 1976 Asian Friendship Invitational Tournament.

In recent years, the European women's teams have also shown steady improvement. The outstanding women table tennis players are from Romania, Yugoslavia, Sweden and the Soviet Union. Most of them are horizontal-racket fast hitters, well trained in the forehand loopspin drive and the backhand serve.

FUNDAMENTALS OF TABLE TENNIS

BECAUSE THE PROPERTIES OF A RACKET WILL, TO a great extent, affect the speed, spin and force of the ball, a good racket is essential even if it does not win a game by itself.

TYPES OF RACKETS

Under the rules of the International Table Tennis Federation, a racket may be covered on either side with pimpled rubber, pips outward, of a total thickness of not more than 2 cm on each side of the blade; or the racket may be sandwiched by a layer of sponge, surfaced with pimpled rubber turned inward or outward, of a total thickness of not more than 4 cm. Three types of racket are most commonly used in competition:

1. *Plain rubber racket*—this racket is covered with a layer of rubber not more than 2 mm in thickness on each side of the wooden blade. It is easy to control. For beginners learning the chop, this racket can be used to aim the ball accurately with little force from the upper arm. However, this racket lacks the "bounceability" of the pips-in or pips-out sponge rackets. It does not produce heavy spins or impart great speed to the ball. Therefore most players who like to attack prefer other rackets.

2. *Pips-out sponge racket*—this racket is covered with pimpled rubber, the pips outward on one or both sides, with a thin layer of sponge sandwiched between the blade and the rubber, total thickness not more than 4 mm. Suitable for the aggressive attacker who can artfully blend the initiative with defense, this racket will produce spins of a velocity unsurpassed by other rackets. Most of our players favor this kind of racket, with small pips over soft sponge.

3. *Pips-in sponge racket*—this racket is made the same way as the pips-out sponge racket, except that the pips are inward and the rubber surface is smooth on the outside. The smoothness produces heavy spins but does not offer the reflexive action or bounce of the pips-out version. Thus, the pips-in model is favored by players who like to use spins. European players generally prefer it. For the attacker, hard

sponge is probably the best interior layer; for the defensive player, soft sponge.

As techniques in table tennis continue to advance, a demand for new and improved rackets is being created. Today there are rubber and sponge rackets made especially to defend against loopspins. Some top-ranked European players also employ rackets with two different surfaces—one side pips-in and the other with oblong rubber dots, giving the racket-holder the option of sides depending on strategy and the type of shot the player anticipates.

RACKET POINTERS

Don't change rackets too often. A player needs time to accustom himself or herself to a racket.

Never blame the racket for a loss. It's the player, not the racket, that's invariably at fault. Even with a good racket, a poor player won't win.

Make sure the handle of the racket fits your hand properly. A poor fit prevents the player from manipulating the racket effectively.

HOW TO RETURN SERVE

To return serve effectively and follow with a succession of attacking strokes, players should learn the following basics:

Judging the incoming ball. By giving close attention to the direction of the stroke by your opponent and how much force is applied to the ball, you can anticipate the kind of spin you will need to neutralize the speed of the ball and the drop point. Here are some fundamental guidelines:

Racket direction	Kind of spin to be anticipated
Forward and downward	Underspin
Upward	Topspin
Left to right	Right sidespin
Right to left	Left Sidespin

You can determine the direction of the ball from the angle of contact between the racket and the ball. For example, if your opponent serves from his right corner, hitting the ball with the racket slanted to his left, the ball will cross the table diagonally and land in your right corner (Diagram 1). From the same position, if your opponent hits the ball square, without angling the racket, the ball will land in your left corner (Diagram 2).

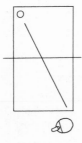

DIAGRAM 1

Diagonal serve

DIAGRAM 2

Straight serve

Carefully observe your opponent's follow-through. Generally, the longer the follow-through, the more powerful the drive, and the more speed and the heavier the spin imparted to the ball.

Foot movement. More likely than not, your opponent will try to direct the ball at a spot as far as possible from where you are positioned. So you should anticipate where the shot will land and be prepared to glide or jump into position to return the ball. Be "springy" on your feet.

Get back to the ready position. After you have returned serve or made your stroke, anticipate your opponent's return and move swiftly back into the ready position. Many points are lost because of a lapse in this fundamental.

UNDERSTANDING SPEED

The close-to-the-table-fast-attack technique of our table tennis players has produced outstanding achievements in international tournaments. The critical factor behind this technique is speed. Studies show our players serve with more speed, initiate swifter attacks and gain positional advantage faster. The advantages of developing speed are thus apparent.

According to the physics of motion:

$$V = \frac{D}{T}, \text{ or Velocity} = \frac{\text{Distance}}{\text{Time}}$$

Applied to table tennis, to accelerate speed you should

1. Stand closer to the table to hit the ball, because the shorter the distance, the less time it takes to return the ball.
2. Hit the ball hard and low with less backswing and a shorter follow-through.
3. Meet the ball while it is still ascending after the bounce. Never wait until the ball is descending, because that gives your opponent more time to react and leaves a less advantageous angle for the ball to clear the net.
4. Exert power in your forearm and wrist when you hit the ball. Here the physics of force (force = mass × speed) are applicable.
5. Develop quick reflexes.

SPINS

Since the advent of the pips-out and pips-in rackets, table tennis players have been refining the game's basic techniques to generate all kinds of spin. Some roll toward you, some away from you, some sideways. Here's how to hit the various spins:

Topspin. At the instant your racket contacts the ball, tilt your racket forward slightly and pull upward and push at the same time (Diagram 3). Topspin rolls forward, toward your opponent. A lot of push-block strokes and attack strokes are hit with topspin.

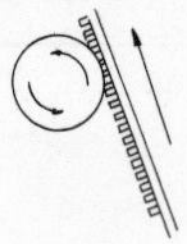

DIAGRAM 3

Topspin

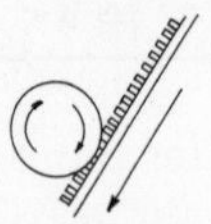

DIAGRAM 4

Underspin

Underspin. At the instant your racket contacts the ball, tilt your racket backward and at the same time shove and push downward (Diagram 4). Underspin rolls away from your opponent. Chops are examples of underspins.

Sidespins. At contact with the ball, if you swing the racket from right to left, you produce a left-to-right sidespin; if you swing from left to right, you produce a right-to-left sidespin (Diagrams 5 and 6).

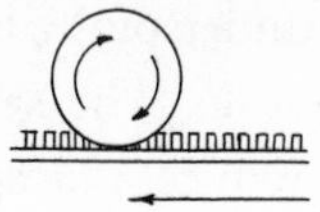

DIAGRAM 5

Left-to-right sidespin

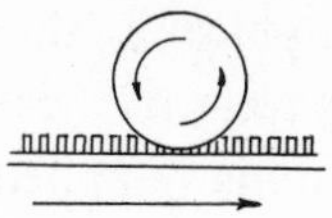

DIAGRAM 6

Right-to-left sidespin

HOW TO RETURN THE VARIOUS SPINS

Topspin and underspin. The air pressure over the top half of a ball hit with topspin forces the ball to fly forward in a low arc. After the ball lands on the table, it bounces low and far. When underspin is applied, the lower half of the ball is deterred by the air, making the ball spin backward and producing a higher arc. After the ball lands, it bounces higher and shorter than a ball hit with topspin (Diagram 7).

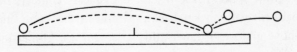

DIAGRAM 7

Dotted line shows path and bounce of topspin. Solid line shows path and bounce of underspin.

After a ball hit with topspin lands on the table, if you contact the ball with your racket held vertically (push-block), the action produces underspin when your return lands on the opponent's side. The same technique applied to underspin produces topspin when your return lands on your opponent's side.

To return topspin, hold your racket slightly tilted forward and contact the middle-upper part of the ball, at the same time pulling upward with some force (Diagram 8). If you want to chop, contact the lower part of the ball with a forward pushing motion.

To return underspin, hold your racket tilted slightly backward and contact the lower part of the ball with a pulling-up-and-forward motion (Diagram 9). If you want to chop, contact the middle of the ball and employ a lot more force to counteract the momentum and change the character of the spin to underspin when the ball lands.

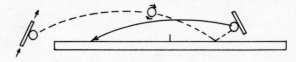

DIAGRAM 8

Racket (right) tilted to return topspin

D<small>IAGRAM</small> 9

Racket (right) tilted to return underspin

Left-to-right sidespin and right-to-left sidespin. If you meet left-to-right sidespin with a straight or vertical racket, the ball will bounce back to the left side of the table on your opponent's side, as you view it (Diagram 10). If you block right-to-left sidespin the same way, the ball will bounce back to the right side of the table on your opponent's side, as you view it (Diagram 11).

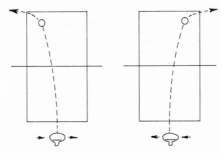

D<small>IAGRAM</small> 10 *(above left)*

Path of the ball after blocking left-to-right sidespin

D<small>IAGRAM</small> 11 *(above right)*

Path of the ball after blocking right-to-left sidespin

To return sidespin, beginners tend to aim left-to-right sidespin toward the right side of the table, as they view it, to prevent the ball from going wide of the table, and vice versa for right-to-left sidespin. However, this is too easily predictable for the opponent. A better way is to wait until the ball is in descent, when the spin is weakest, then hit the ball with force, aiming it wherever you want your return to land.

ACCELERATING SPIN

If you hit a ball directly upward with a racket held horizontally, the ball will bounce but not spin (Diagram 12). However, if at the same time, you rub the ball either from left to right or from right to left, you create spin (Diagram 13).

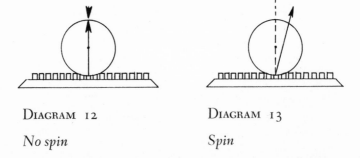

DIAGRAM 12

No spin

DIAGRAM 13

Spin

According to physics, the motion of the spin is determined by the friction between the racket and the ball, and the degree of the spin is determined by the accelerating force from the arm. Therefore, to create spin:

1. The point at which you make contact with the ball should be either at the uppermost part of the ball or at the lowermost part, never at the center of the ball.
2. At the point of contact, accelerate with speed and force.
3. Choose a racket with a texture that generates friction for spins and has soft sponge for bounceability.

By fully understanding the physics of spins, modern table tennis players have experimented and combined all kinds of spin to improve their technique. In recent years, they have developed the loop, and that stroke has become an important element in championship competition and improved the level of play enormously.

Teaching & Training

TABLE TENNIS AS A RECREATION

CHAIRMAN MAO SAID THAT OUR EDUCATORS SHOULD aim at developing young people's ethics, intelligence and physical fitness so that the young will become conscientious members of a socialistic society. During their growing and habit-forming years, young people should not overlook the importance of physical fitness. Training in table tennis for young people after work and for children after school is a way to promote interest in physical fitness and body building, and to lay a good foundation for perfecting the techniques and upgrading the standard of table tennis.

MENTAL APPROACH TO TRAINING

Learn from the ideology of Marx-Lenin and Chairman Mao's teachings, the ultimate goal being to serve the country and manifest the socialistic ideology by striving to reach the pinnacle of excellence in sports.

Study and practice the techniques. Learn not only the close-to-the-table-fast-attack technique as a fundamental tactic, but also the techniques of players from other countries. Do not neglect the defensive techniques such as the chop to parry an attack and develop an opening to launch a counterattack.

FUNDAMENTAL TRAINING PRINCIPLES

Combine the correct mental approach with training in tactics and physical conditioning exercises. Follow the slogan: "Friendship first, competition second."

Combine training in basics with simultaneous physical training. Do not neglect body building and physical conditioning exercises. A sound body is the foundation for all sports.

With general physical exercises, incorporate special exercises to develop various parts of the body for special needs.

Plan a basic training program for the varying levels of technique. A coach should give special attention to individual needs and assign appropriate programs for each individual.

The physical capability of each player should dictate what training program the player should follow. Young children, for example, should not do strenuous exercises. Overexertion can cause injuries. It is the coach's responsibility to determine what is best for each player, taking into consideration age, size and build. As young players grow, expanded training programs may be recommended.

TRAINING
FOR BEGINNERS

UNDER CHAIRMAN MAO'S REVOLUTIONARY PHYSICAL education guidelines, table tennis became the most popular national sport in China and advanced at a remarkable pace toward higher standards. Table tennis facilities were made available to everyone. Children used to begin playing at age nine or ten (in third or fourth grade). Now the age is down to seven or eight (in first or second grade). It has been proven that the younger children begin training, the better the foundation.

Generally, youngsters are required to pass the following three basic tests:

1. Demonstrate a knowledge of the fundamentals of the forehand attack (straight or cross-court), push, block, pull and chop.
2. Possess the stamina to return the ball at least 10 to 20 times.
3. Demonstrate a knowledge of the correct hand and foot movements.

Usually, beginners can pass the three tests after one or two years of training.

HOW TO HOLD THE RACKET

It is important for a beginner to learn how to hold the racket correctly right from the start. Basically, there are two ways to hold the racket: vertically or horizontally. Each way has its advantages and disadvantages. The vertical method is more suitable for the close-to-the-table-fast-hit attacker and makes it easier to push-block for the defensive player. The horizontal method affords a wider range of action and is more suitable for the player who likes to use backhand strokes. Here are the four most common methods of holding the racket:

1. *Vertical attack style* (Diagram 14)—hold the racket as you would a pencil, resting the thumb on the front of the racket with the top two joints of the forefinger hooked over the handle like a clamp, finger and thumb about 2 cm apart. At the back, the first joint of the middle finger rests sideways on the racket

at the center, and the other two fingers rest on the middle finger.

2. *Vertical defense style* (Diagram 15)—the bottom half of the thumb rests on the front of the racket and the four fingers are spread over the back of the racket.

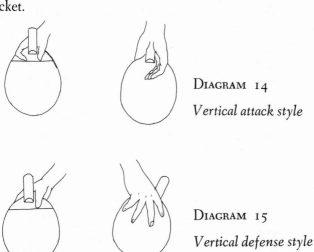

Diagram 14

Vertical attack style

Diagram 15

Vertical defense style

3. *Horizontal attack style* (Diagram 16)—hold the racket as you would a cleaver. The thumb is stretched diagonally over the front of the racket, the forefinger is diagonal over the back of the racket, and the other three fingers hold the handle.

4. *Horizontal defense style* (Diagram 17)—the racket is held in a manner similar to the horizontal attack style, except that the forefinger is bent closer to the middle finger and the thumb is placed farther down on the blade. The grip is also loose enough to allow easy movement.

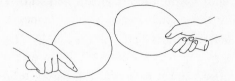

DIAGRAM 16

Horizontal attack style

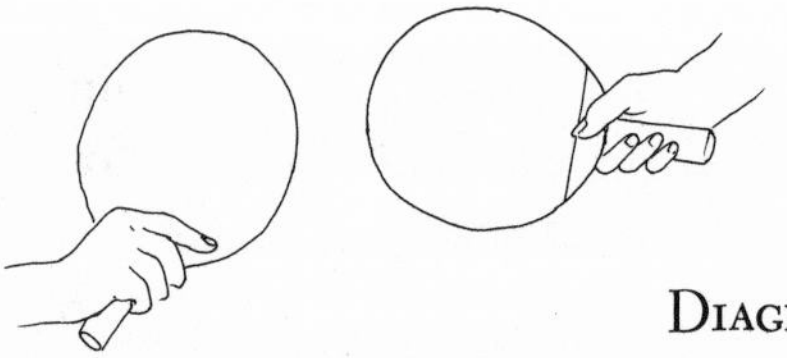

DIAGRAM 17

Horizontal defense style

GRIP POINTERS

Avoid gripping the handle too tightly or too loosely. Too tight a grip hinders wrist movement. Too loose a grip makes the racket unsteady.

The relationship between the fingers and the racket should be such that the fingers can maneuver the racket freely. For the drive, the vertical racket holder relies on the three fingers in back to steady the racket while the thumb presses down hard. For the backhand push-block, the forefinger presses hard on the racket for a firm grip and control while the middle finger exerts the force. The horizontal racket holder uses the forefinger to control the racket for a forehand attack and the thumb to control the racket for the backhand attack, keeping the middle finger loose to maneuver the racket in both instances.

The relationship between the racket and the wrist is important. The vertical racket holder getting ready to attack holds the racket straight out, like an extension of the arm. This position allows the force to flow easily through the wrist to the racket. The horizontal racket holder, on the other hand, lifts or cocks the wrist a little.

Learn to relax the arm muscles. Don't strain the fingers by gripping the racket too tightly before or after you make contact. Vertical racket holders tend to make two mistakes. The first is leaving too big a space between the thumb and forefinger, which hinders wrist movement. That space should be no more than 2 cm. The second mistake is spreading the last two fingers over the back of the racket, instead of resting them on the middle finger. This hinders the backhand action.

BALL BEHAVIOR

All beginners should go through exercises that help them to understand the behavior of the ball. Here are some of the best exercises:

Hold the racket face at abdomen level. Bounce the ball gently off the racket face, not too high at first, then alternately increase and decrease force. Next, continue to bounce the ball while moving your feet left, right, forward and backward. For beginners, the ball may be attached to a string initially.

Practice hitting the ball against a wall. Hold the racket tilted slightly backward and stand about 80 cm to 100 cm from the wall. Practice hitting two ways: after the ball bounces from the floor and then before it lands on the floor. Don't let the ball bounce higher than your head. Try to minimize the target area on the wall. Learn to control the bounce from high to low. Move around while hitting the ball.

Practice hitting the ball into the air with another player, first from a stationary position and then while moving around.

Place a table next to the wall and practice hitting the ball against the wall so that it bounces on the table.

Practice hitting the ball back and forth on a table tennis table with another player.

COORDINATING HAND AND FOOT MOVEMENTS

While the beginner is doing exercises to learn more about the behavior of the ball, exercises to coordinate the movement of the hands and feet should begin simultaneously. Correct posture is important. Stand with the feet parallel, about the width of the shoulders apart, heels slightly off the floor, knees bent slightly inward, the upper body tilted slightly forward. This posture relaxes the muscles and prepares the body for action. Never stand with your toes pointed outward because that causes muscle tension in the back and sets the body weight on the heels, which hinders movement. Hand and foot movement exercises may be grouped under the following headings:

To attack:

(a) Forehand drive or attack
(b) Push-block
(c) Single-step push-block
(d) Single-step backhand push and forehand drive
(e) Two-step jump-over backhand push and forehand drive
(f) Quick one-step jump-over backhand push and forehand drive
(g) Push-block attack, standing sideways
(h) Push-block smash attack, standing sideways, with a quick one-step jump-over back to the original position

For defense:

(a) Forehand drive
(b) Backhand drive
(c) Forehand and backhand short chop
(d) Forehand and backhand chop, single-step
(e) Forehand chop, followed by a short kill shot with a quick jump-over step
(f) Backhand chop followed by a short kill shot with a quick jump-over step

Forehand drive

Right-handers stand with the left foot slightly forward, left-handers with the right foot slightly forward. The racket-holding arm stretches sideways about 35 to 40 degrees from the body and is bent, with the angle between the upper arm and forearm about 120 degrees. The racket is tilted backward slightly, except when you're using a pips-in racket, in which case do not tilt the racket. The weight is on the right foot, if you're a right-hander, with the body turned slightly to the right. If you're a left-hander, the weight is on the left foot with the body turned slightly to the left. To make the stroke right-handed, using force from your forearm swing the racket forward toward the upper left in a short arc, turning the wrist to tilt the racket forward. At the same time, pivot your body to the left and shift your weight to the left foot from the right foot. At the end of the follow-through, the racket should be near your face, then quickly returned to the ready position.

Push-blocking

The stance, for right-handers, has the left foot forward; for left-handers, the right foot forward. Set the feet parallel to each other and bend the knees. Hold the upper arm and elbow of the racket-holding hand close to your body—the angle between the upper arm and forearm should be about 100 degrees—with the forearm in front of the abdomen holding the racket in a horizontal position. The racket face should be perpendicular to the table. To make the stroke, exert force with your forearm and wrist, pushing the racket forward and downward. After hitting, return to the ready position quickly.

Forehand chop (horizontal racket holder)

The right foot is forward, the knees are bent and the feet are parallel to each other. The upper arm of the racket-holding hand is slightly away from the body with the forearm bent upward, the racket handle pointing diagonally down, about 20 cm to 30 cm in front of the hip. To make the stroke, move the right foot back half a step, with the body tilted slightly forward and the weight moving to the right foot. Stretch your hitting arm out—the upper arm and the forearm should be at a right angle—tilt the racket backward, then move your upper arm back and swing your forearm leftward and downward in an arc, at the same time pivoting the body and shifting the weight to the left foot (Diagram 18). After hitting, return to the ready position.

DIAGRAM 18

Forehand chop (horizontal racket holder)

Backhand chop (horizontal racket holder)

The stance is the same as for the forehand chop, except that, for right-handers, the left foot is half a step back of the right foot, the body leans toward the left and the weight is on the left foot. The right forearm is in front of the chest—the angle between the upper arm and the forearm should be about 70 degrees—and the racket handle points diagonally down. To make the stroke, activate force in your forearm and move the whole arm up toward your left shoulder, swinging the racket from the upper left down in an arc toward your lower right while pivoting the body and shifting your weight to your right foot (Diagram 19). At the completion of the follow-through, the racket is waist-high and your left foot moves back to the original stance.

DIAGRAM 19

Backhand chop (horizontal racket holder)

Single-step foot movement

Depending on the direction of the incoming ball, move one step with one foot and pivot on the other foot in the same direction to meet the ball (Diagram 20).

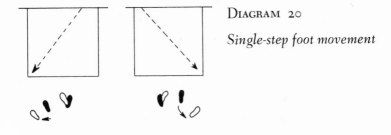

DIAGRAM 20

Single-step foot movement

Two-step jump-over

Sometimes, when your opponent's shot is placed at a spot far from where you are positioned, you can reach the ball only by quickly jumping over, moving one foot after the other (Diagram 21).

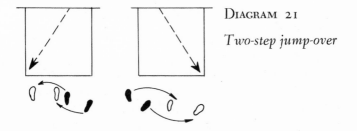

DIAGRAM 21

Two-step jump-over

Quick jump-over

Depending on the direction of the incoming ball, to meet the ball in time, you need to jump over quickly, either to the left or to the right, moving both feet almost simultaneously (Diagram 22).

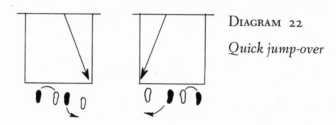

DIAGRAM 22

Quick jump-over

HOW TO HIT THE BASIC STROKES

Serving

The simplest and most basic serve is the forehand drive. The right-hander stands with both feet parallel, the left foot slightly forward and the body turned slightly to the right. The ball is held in the palm of the left hand, the right hand holding the racket in front of the body. Toss the ball in the air and, as it falls, swing your right arm, aiming to hit the middle part of the ball. Make contact after the ball bounces on your side of the table.

Blocking

Blocking is the simplest way to meet an oncoming ball. You simply reverse the force of the ball by placing the blade of your racket in front of the ball. Don't tilt the racket too much either forward or backward, because a tilted racket will cause the ball to bounce too low or too high. Remember to incorporate the appropriate hand and foot movements.

DIAGRAM 23

Press-down push-block

Push-blocking technique

When blocking an oncoming ball, use a little force to push as the ball ascends. Because push-blocking requires only slight motion to control an oncoming ball, a player can return the ball unpredictably to an opponent and develop a positional advantage. Beginners should learn how to hit underspin push-blocks to deal with fast-spin serves. The technique is to stand about 30 cm to 40 cm from the table, the left foot slightly forward if you are right-handed. The forearm rests on the abdomen, with an angle of about 100 degrees between the upper arm and forearm. The racket is tilted backward about 80 degrees from the table. Aim to make contact with the upper-middle part of the ball while the ball is still ascending. If the oncoming ball bounces high, tilt your racket forward and push down hard to exert force (Diagram 23). This technique is especially suitable for tall players.

If the incoming ball is characterized by loopspin, slide your racket from right to left as you push-block (Diagram 24). This calls for a fast and delicate wrist maneuver, but it's a useful technique every beginner should learn.

DIAGRAM 24

Fast push-block with slide from right to left

To exert a strong push, loosen the pressure of your thumb and press hard with the forefinger. Use the middle finger in back of the racket to tilt the racket to compensate for the degree of spin of the oncoming ball. If the spin is weak topspin, tilt the racket forward only a little. If the spin is loopspin, contact the upper part of the ball. The ideal moment to start your stroke is when the ball is 15 cm from your racket. You lose both momentum and speed if you start when the ball is farther away, and you will have difficulty maneuvering accurately if the ball is too close.

Foot movements. Most push-blocks call for the single-step foot movement. Do not stretch to reach the oncoming ball. Instead, move your feet to where you can push-block without extending your arm. After hitting the shot, get back to the ready position with a quick jump-over.

Push-blocking pointers: Don't start to push too soon. That reduces the force of your shots.

Coordinate your foot movements with your hand movements.

Make sure your finger manipulations on the racket are not premature or belated.

Don't take too long a follow-through. It could leave you out of position to return your opponent's next shot.

Intensive practice routines

Have someone serve to various parts of the left court while you try to return serve quickly, remembering to coordinate your foot movements with your strokes.

Practice hitting balls attack-style to various spots in the opponent's left court without the ball bouncing on your side of the table.

Combine the two foregoing exercises.

Practice returning a short serve from the left side of the table to two different spots.

Toss the balls yourself and practice push-blocking.

Practice routines with a coach or more experienced player.

Push-block to various parts of the table, concentrating on maneuvering the racket to hit the ball straight and diagonally.

Push-block from one side of the table only, reaching the position with agile foot movements.

Push-block diagonally and then change to straight shots.

Push-block against a group of opponents who take turns hitting the ball back.

Push-block diagonally several times, then vary the direction of your shots.

Push-block while standing sideways.

Exercises for beginners. Push-block diagonally and then straight.

Hit push and attack shots alternately.

Push-block in various directions.

Training under game conditions. Give each player 10 to 20 balls to serve to a designated spot on the table and keep a record of the players' accuracy.

Establish a time limit for each player to hit a fixed number of push and attack shots, keeping each player's statistics.

Give numerical designations to four tables before starting competition. The winners advance toward table #1 and the losers fall back toward table #4.

Backhand fast-hit serve (horizontal racket holder)

After mastering the technique of blocking, the horizontal racket holder should learn the backhand fast-hit serve, the foundation for double-attack tactics. The force and speed are quite effective, and can actually intimidate some opponents.

The force comes mainly from the wrist, which accelerates as well as reverses the force of the ball by contacting the upper part of the ball as it ascends (Diagram 25). The wrist controls the racket and the direction by tilting forward or backward, to right or left, or any combination of those, depending on the force of the ball and the degree of spin. Through practice, a player can learn how much force to apply and the proper angle to tilt the racket. The horizontal racket holder does not push like the vertical racket holder but moves the wrist forward to the right (for a right-hander) to hit cross-court, or straight forward to hit straight. Also, the racket should be tilted more

DIAGRAM 25

Backhand fast-hit serve (horizontal racket holder)

for a heavy spin and less for a weaker spin. The stance is the same as the vertical racket holder's, but the horizontal racket holder must remember not to bend the wrist inward. The foot movements and training meanwhile are the same as for push-blocking.

DIAGRAM 26

Forehand drive underspin

Forehand drive

The forehand drive is a technique modern, aggressive players use to win a point quickly. Therefore it should become part of everyone's basic training routine. That includes learning how to impart topspin and underspin and how to execute the smash or kill shot.

Topspin is used to counteract underspins such as chops that rotate away from the player. The technique is to contact the lower part of an oncoming ball as it descends, with the racket tilted slightly backward. Use a pull-up motion. That will convert the underspin into topspin when the ball lands on your opponent's side of the table.

Underspin is used to counteract topspin, push-blocking or any ball that bounces into your body. The technique is to meet the ball as it ascends with the racket tilted slightly forward. Contact the upper part of the ball with a slice-down motion (Diagram 26). That changes topspin to underspin.

The smash or kill shot is utilized when your opponent hits a ball that bounces much higher than the net. With the racket straight and perpendicular to the table, swing your arm back and then forward with force, aiming at the middle of the ball, using a wrist snap to knock the ball out of the reach of your opponent.

The accompanying chart shows the relationship among body, hand and foot movements in executing topspin, underspin and the smash or kill shot.

	Topspin	*Underspin*	*Smash or Kill Shot*
Body distance from table	About 50 cm to 60 cm Left foot slightly forward	About 20 cm to 30 cm Both feet parallel	About 40 cm to 50 cm Left foot forward, standing sideways
Angle between body and upper arm	$40°$ to $50°$ Forearm parallel to floor	$30°$ to $40°$	$70°$ to $90°$
Angle between upper arm and forearm	$130°$ Elbow slightly back	$120°$ Elbow slightly back	$150°$ to $160°$
Racket tilt	Tilted backward $100°$ to $120°$ Thumb pressure on front, palm faces upward	Tilted forward $70°$ to $80°$ Thumb pressure on front, palm faces downward	Almost perpendicular to floor, palm toward front
The stroke	Move the upper arm back, swing forward and down, contacting ball about 30 cm from right waist with a pull-up rub, the wrist exerting force to accelerate spin; after hitting, follow through so that the racket winds up in front of forehead	Swing the forearm (pivoting at elbow) and upper arm, meeting ball at a slightly higher level than topspin and more than 30 cm from body, the wrist and fingers angling the direction; after hitting, racket finishes in front of face	Move the arm back and swing forward, whip with force; body pivots from side to front and to left; as the racket hits the ball, the arm is higher than for underspin, about 40 cm from body, the wrist controlling the direction; after hitting, the racket finishes in front of chest

In developing the forehand drive, beginners should pay special attention to the following points:

(a) Use wrist force to return short shots that remain inside the table, exert forearm force for close-to-the-table shots, and use upper arm force for deep shots.

(b) Counteract topspin with a low-arc return and underspin with a high-arc return.

Training routine. Practice the forehand drive stroking action without the ball, coordinating your hand and foot movements. Keep your feet on the move—agile foot movement is the foundation for the shot. Also learn to accelerate the force of your shots, using your body, legs and arm.

Have someone serve balls to designated spots on your side of the table and return each serve with a forehand drive.

Place your left hand over your right elbow to make sure the elbow is not held too high. Place the palm of your left hand under your right underarm to keep the upper part of your right arm from resting too close to the body. If you're left-handed, use your right hand to assist in the exercises.

In practicing return of serve, have the server gradually increase the speed of the serve so that you develop your reflexes. For the player who has the bad habit of moving the upper arm too much, or is too stiff-wristed, practice returning short shots. For the player whose foot movement is sluggish, work on returning placements.

Place a bench behind you so that you are obliged to

stand close to the table. This will help you to learn the close-to-the-table-fast-hit technique.

Rotate the exercises. Don't overdo any one exercise.

Avoid taking too much backswing or making the follow-through too long. Don't let the wrist and racket hang downward like an eagle claw—this is detrimental to the force of your shots. And don't let your chest or stomach stick out or let your feet become static.

Forehand fast-hit underspin

Training routine. Practice the stroke without a ball, at the same time employing the single-step, two-step jump-over and quick jump-over foot movements.

Practice the push-blocking exercises.

Assemble five or six players and line them up to take turns running to the table to return the ball successively. Such group practice sharpens anticipation, decision-making and ball sense, and also develops foot movement.

Practice with a defensive player who returns the ball largely by push-blocking, giving you a chance to execute a succession of attack shots to one spot or to launch placement shots to various spots.

Try a few forehand attack shots diagonally to your opponent's right court, gradually increasing the speed and frequency of the shots. Then mix in a few straight backhand shots. Work on the quick jump-over and the single-step or the two-step jump-over.

Also practice push-blocking while standing sideways, increasing the speed and force of your strokes progressively.

Arrange a series of matches from time to time to determine how effectively the players are acquiring the techniques. Keep a record of each player's performance.

Forehand topspin and smash

Training routine. Without a ball, practice the motion for the forehand drive, coordinating the stroke with foot movement exercises.

With a partner, practice the forehand topspin technique, beginning with a few diagonal shots. Then practice the close-to-the-table-fast-hit attack strokes. With a chopper as your opponent, practice placement shots diagonally to the left and right, concentrating on accuracy. After mastering the basic techniques, with a coach or more advanced player practice the placement attack strokes, hitting to two spots. Finally, combine the forehand topspin with the smash or kill shot. You can throw the ball yourself and smash or have someone serve the ball for you to smash.

Short chops

The short chop is a useful tactic against underspin and to weather a crisis while you maneuver into position for a counterattack. It can also be a quick point-getter if a player learns how to execute the stroke to perfection. The short chop can be used effectively with push-blocking or combined with other attack techniques.

Fundamentals. Stand about 40 cm behind the table with the left foot slightly forward. For the fast short chop, contact the middle part of the ball at the peak of its ascent. For the slow short chop, contact the lower part of the ball as it descends. Make a short follow-through, using force from the forearm and wrist. For the backhand chop, the forearm is slanted and the force is mainly from a snap or flick of the wrist.

For the fast short chop, the racket is held tilted slightly backward. After hitting, the racket is flat. If the oncoming ball has a strong spin, at contact tilt the tip of the racket up slightly with your wrist. For the slow short chop, meet the oncoming ball with your racket tilted back to almost flat, the racket remaining that way after hitting. The motion for the forehand fast short chop is a slice-down rub. You swing from your right side in toward the oncoming ball with the racket tilted slightly backward. As you contact the ball at the peak of its ascent you can regulate the amount of spin you impart to the ball with your wrist and the force from your forearm (Diagram 27).

DIAGRAM 27

Forehand slice

The backhand short chop is more of a shoveling action. You move your racket from your lower chest forward to shove the ball back, again working off a slice-down rub (Diagram 28). The follow-through is shorter than for the forehand slice.

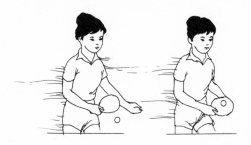

DIAGRAM 28

Backhand shove

Be careful not to hold the racket too tightly or to tilt the racket too far back, or you'll hit the wrong part of the ball.

Guard against shifting the racket to the side rather than slicing or shoving forward and downward.

Learn how to maneuver the racket so you can utilize the spin of the incoming ball.

Training routine. Practice the motion of the basic stroke without a ball. Learn how to exert forearm force and to maneuver the attitude of the racket with wrist control.

Throw the balls yourself to practice the basic stroke.

Have someone serve underspins for you to practice returns.

Have someone throw the balls to you to hit.

Practice in a group of two or more players, hitting forehand and backhand short chops.

Have someone serve spins, nonspins, fast short chops and slow short chops for you to return.

Practice returning all kinds of placements. Return them either straight or diagonally by angling the racket and using wrist control. Learn how to use the fore-arm and wrist to return the ball short or deep.

Divide the opponent's side of the table into nine sections. Number each section. Return the ball to a numbered section designated by the coach.

Practice with a partner. Start with the backhand shove, hitting straight and diagonal shots, then short and deep shots and finally fast and slow short chops. Practice the forehand slice with the same variations.

Finally, play against two or three players lined up to take turns, running in to the table to hit alternately.

Chopping

The chop is an important technique in defense as well as for counterattacking. By reversing the force and spin of the oncoming ball, the chopper varies his strokes, applying spin to some balls and not to others. Or the chopper can use placements to gain positional advantage and upset an opponent's equilibrium, ulti-mately mounting an attack. To be a good chopper, a player must build up physical stamina for endur-ance and perseverance. The player must also have quick reflexes, good coordination, agility in hand and foot movements, and the mental stability to keep calm under attack while preparing to launch a counterattack.

Forehand chop. If you're a right-hander, stand with the left foot slightly forward of the right foot, slightly bent at the waist, body angled to the right. The forearm is bent upward so that there is an angle of almost 90 degrees between the upper arm and the forearm. Hold the racket with the face flat at the level of your shoulder. After hitting the ball, the racket finishes horizontal in front of the abdomen with the handle aligned with the forearm. Try to contact the lower half of the ball as it descends. To make the stroke, swing your arm back and then forward and downward in an arc, pivoting at the waist on the follow-through. The arc after hitting is longer than the arc before hitting.

Backhand chop. Right-handers stand with the right foot forward, body turned toward the left, the weight on the left foot. The right upper arm is close to the chest with the forearm pointed upward. The angle between the upper arm and the lower arm is about 70 degrees. Before making contact, the racket is face up with the handle pointed down, level with the left shoulder. After contact, the racket winds up in front of the right side of the body, waist-high and close to the body. Contact the lower-middle part of the ball as it descends. Use forearm force to whip down and forward in a semicircle as you meet the ball, at the same time employing the wrist to angle the ball and accelerate underspin.

Footwork. Footwork is one of the decisive factors in any game. Agility in foot movement gives a chopper confidence and the initiative in competition. Beginners should practice the single-step and the two-step jump-over for the short chop and the quick jump-over and the crossover step for the deep chop. Make sure you return to the ready position after the stroke and be prepared to move your feet for the next shot.

Training routine. In intensive practice, work on both the forehand and backhand chops and on returning the ball with spin to designated spots.

With a coach, practice the forehand and backhand, hitting placements short and deep, and also attack strokes or kill shots. Coordinate the proper hand and foot movements with the strokes.

With a partner, practice the chopping technique to create an attack unexpectedly. Hit to designated spots and vary these shots with unexpected placements.

Make sure you don't take too big a backswing. Don't overextend the follow-through after hitting, either. That loses time before you can return to the ready position for the next shot. Coordinate the wrist movement with the movement of the forearm to avoid unwanted spins and prevent your return from flying too high.

DIAGRAM 29
The stance

1   2

Side view   *Front view*

1   2

DIAGRAM 30
Movements to practice as the coach calls the numbers

56

DIAGRAM 31
Push-blocking as the coach calls the numbers

1   2   Side views

3   4   5

Front views

Diagram 32

Single-step push-block (1 and 2) and back to ready position (3 and 4)

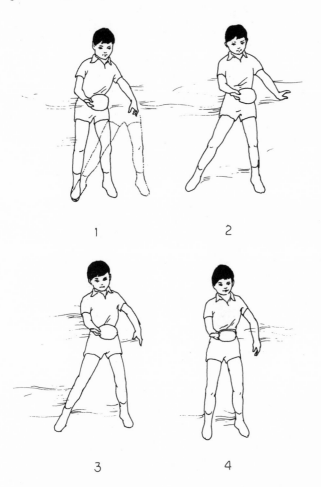

1   2

3   4

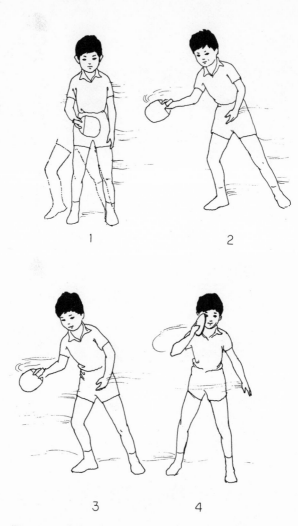

1

2

3

4

DIAGRAM 33

Single-step backhand push/forehand attack

Follow the exercise in Diagram 32 with the forehand stroke (above) and return to the ready position (1).

DIAGRAM 34

Two-step jump-over backhand push/forehand attack

Follow the exercise in Diagram 30 with the two-step jump-over backhand push/forehand attack (above) and return to the ready position (5).

1   2   3

4   5

Diagram 35

Quick jump-over backhand push/forehand attack

Follow the exercise in Diagram 31 with the quick jump-over backhand push/forehand attack (above) and return to the ready position (5).

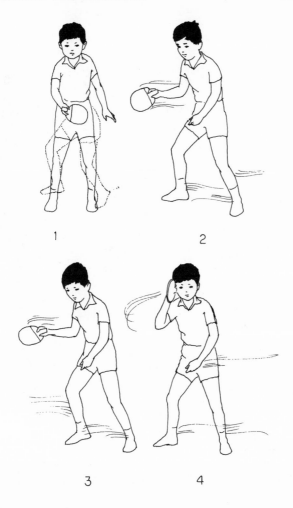

1

2

3

4

DIAGRAM 36

Forehand push-block while standing sideways

Follow the exercise in Diagram 31 with the forehand push-block while standing sideways (above) and return to the ready position (1).

62

1   2   3

4   5

DIAGRAM 37

Forehand push-block smash while standing sideways

Follow the exercise in Diagram 31 with the exercise in Diagram 36 and then the forehand push-block smash (above), then return to the ready position (5).

STRATEGIC TRAINING

AFTER ONE TO TWO YEARS OF BASIC TRAINING, THE player is ready for advanced training. A coach should determine the type of advanced training suitable for each individual, taking into consideration the player's weak and strong points. Advanced training should follow a step-by-step progression to build a strong foundation from which each player can develop a style of play.

Advanced training generally covers five years. Most participants in China are between eleven and sixteen years old. Besides the four main strategic training techniques—backhand push/forehand attack, double attack, loop drive, and chop—training also covers serving and returning serve. At this time, the players are taught tactics as well as techniques. Usually, a player will spend one or two years specializing in one or two sets of strategic strokes for attacking and also for defense.

Following are the strategic training techniques for advanced players:

BACKHAND PUSH/FOREHAND ATTACK

This is a traditional strategy developed by China's vertical racket holders after years of rigid training in combining different techniques and tactics. The player stands close to the table and is in an advantageous position to hit the ball hard and with direction to put pressure on an opponent's weak side. The advantage of this strategy is that the player has good control. By push-blocking, the player can maneuver the ball to apply pressure or use loopspins. When there is an opening, the player can launch a succession of forehand drives with accelerating speed.

Avoid

Executing the attack stroke while standing sideways when you should be using the forehand drive

Standing too far back from the table, which gives your opponent a chance to attack

Passivity in blocking loopspins

Moving your feet too slowly

Failing to return to the ready position

Using too many short chops, instead of the more effective backhand push/forehand drive

Players should strive to develop a style of attacking based on topspin and speed, rather than just aiming to win a point. Of equal importance is knowing how and when to employ loopspin.

The backhand push/forehand attack technique is based on three main tactics:

1. Push-block a few times, then suddenly turn sideways for a kill shot.

2. Use backhand push-blocks to put pressure on an opponent's weak side, then suddenly turn sideways to slam a fast forehand drive. This is especially suitable for a tall player who is not swift afoot. A coach may want to consider training the tall player in this procedure first, but generally players should start with procedure No. 1.

3. Using a pips-in sponge racket, combine the backhand push/forehand attack with loopspins. Loopspin is effective against underspin. The loopdrive often yields a positional advantage.

Foot movement

The area of foot movement in table tennis is, of course, much wider than the table. So players must be agile. Practice the three basic foot movements: (1) single-step, (2) two-step jump-over, (3) quick jump-over. Players should also develop the foot movements to execute a stroke while standing slightly sideways, right-handers pivoting on the left foot while the right foot moves backward and the body is turned slightly to the right. After hitting the ball, return to the ready position with a quick jump-over and be prepared for the next stroke.

To execute a stroke standing sideways, the footwork is a two-step jump-over. The left foot moves a small step to the left, followed by the right foot moving back one big step, about a meter from the table. Return to the original position immediately by pivoting on the right foot.

For the smash shot, use the crossover step. The first step should be shorter so that the other foot can cross over to execute the smash. The direction of the crossover step is toward the side rather than backward. After hitting the ball, use the quick jump-over step to return to the ready position.

The foot movements are of fundamental importance and should be practiced constantly, first stressing co-ordination, second reflexes and third agility.

Push-block training

To give your push strokes acceleration, meet the oncoming ball at the peak of its ascent. The upper arm should be slightly back, forearm holding the racket high. Anticipate the type of ball you are going to receive, and angle your racket accordingly. Meet the lower part of the ball and push the racket downward with the three fingers in back of the racket. The racket should be held steady so you can push accurately.

To counteract underspin, hit the lower-middle part of the ball. The stroke is the same as the regular action of push-blocking. At ball contact, don't ease up on your thumb pressure or move your wrist. The thumb, in fact, should apply a little pressure on the racket to retain the angle. Exert force, pushing forward to prevent the ball from flying too high.

To capitalize on a weak oncoming ball, don't always hit a hard shot. Instead, try a soft drop shot on occasion. It might catch your opponent off guard.

How to improve your forehand drive

After reviewing the fundamentals of fast-hit play, the loop drive, the kill shot and placements, the player should learn to combine two of these strategies. The combination might be the close-to-the-table attack followed by the away-from-the-table attack, the fast-hit attack followed by a kill shot, loopdrives with a kill shot, or a smash shot after a few attack shots while standing sideways.

Training for the backhand push/ forehand attack

Concentrate on forehand fast-serving and attacking, backhand pushing for defense, and agility in foot movements covering the forehand court.

For defense, practice backhand pushing with placements to two different targets. For attacking, practice a succession of forehand shots. Coordinate them with foot movement exercises.

Hit backhand pushes to various parts of the table.

Follow an exchange of push-blocks with a surprise forehand attack shot while standing sideways. Have a partner serve several balls to your backhand court, then have the partner suddenly switch to your forehand court to give you the opportunity to execute a forehand attack while standing sideways.

Practice hitting the ball with increased force to your opponent's forehand court a few times, then concentrate on accelerating the speed and hitting to the opponent's backhand court. Whenever the opponent is in a defensive position, accelerate the speed of your forehands to the opponent's backhand court.

Combine backhand pushing and push-blocking with a forehand attack executed while standing sideways, using a smash shot. Have a partner serve a few balls for backhand pushing and push-blocking, then to your forehand court to enable you to practice the attack and smash shots. Work on coordination, reflexes and agility. Next, concentrate on speed in executing a succession of forehand drives while standing sideways, followed by a smash or kill shot.

Practice with a backhand-style player. Put pressure on your opponent by accelerating your forehand drives.

Use the backhand push/forehand attack strategy against loopspin shots.

Practice backhand push-blocking to return the ball diagonally to the opponent's backhand court, then hit a forehand drive while standing sideways to return a loopspin shot. Many players have no difficulty returning a loopspin with a backhand push, but returning a loopspin with a forehand drive calls for practice to perfect the technique. It is an important and fundamental maneuver that every good player should be psychologically prepared to master. Remember: a loopspin has heavy spin and forward momentum, so you need to tilt your racket slightly toward the net. Aim to contact the ascending ball with force from your forearm. Near the end of your stroke, accelerate the force with a downward wrist snap.

Short chops, rubs and counterattack tactics

When your opponent gives you a ball with heavy underspin near the net, meet the ball with a rubbing or grazing action to convert the spin into a topspin return. The rub is a delicate motion, and a player needs to learn to keep the stroke fast, short and low. For a counterattack, the strategy is to plan a succession of spins to the opponent's backhand court followed by a forehand shot short, near the net. To practice, players should start with backhand short chops. After a few exchanges, try to maneuver into a counterattack or a sudden kill shot.

With a chopper, practice spins, drop shots and smash shots. You will meet defensive players like the chopper often in competition. Therefore it's worthwhile to learn how to deal with a chopper's shots, mainly underspins that you need not hit as hard as you would an attacker's shots. Spins, drop shots and smash shots are good tactics against a chop. The spins should have speed and be angled to the side. If you use an inverted pips-in racket, you can incorporate some loopspins into your tactics. The drop shots should be low and short. They call for good coordination and suppleness in the wrist. The smash, meanwhile, is a quick point-winning technique. Learn to counteract spins, and when you get a short, low ball near the net, smash it at the apex of the bounce.

Lobbing

The lob is a passive tactic to deal with a crisis when you are under attack. The shot is normally hit well back from the table, about two meters behind it. To make the stroke, hold the racket flat and parallel to the floor. Meet the ball as it descends. Depending on how high and far you want to lob, angle the arc to control the flight. Practice lobbing with a partner who will hit the ball back to you. After lobbing a few times, plan a counterattack before your opponent hits a point-winner.

Practicing loopspins with a pips-in sponge racket

Combine the loopspins with the backhand push/ forehand attack strategy. Practice accuracy first, then concentrate on spins, especially underspins, and loop-spins from the forehand side, combining the loop-spins with the serve and returning the serve with loopspin.

Backhand push/forehand attack strategy

Forehand fast serve. Most forehand fast serves are appropriate for developing the backhand push/fore-hand attack strategy. The advantage of the forehand fast serve is that the speed of the ball and the short follow-through help to mask your placements and leave your opponent uncertain. The secret of the fast serve is in the wrist maneuver. At the moment the racket contacts the ball, you can apply topspin or underspin, or impart direction so subtly that it's hard for your opponent to pick up.

Attacking after returning serve. With quick reflexes and accurate placements, returning the serve can be a prelude to attacking. The pips-in racket player, for example, can return the serve with loopspins and follow with more attack strokes.

How to deal with a forehand-and-backhand attack

Push-block to the opponent's midsection, or while standing sideways, fast-hit or push-block to a spot beyond the reach of your opponent.

Fast-hit a few hard strokes to the opponent's backhand court, then suddenly change tactics and hit some balls to the middle of the opponent's forehand court. The speed of the transition is critical. If you do it fast enough, you might be able to force your opponent to move back and leave an opening for you to hit a point-winner.

Push-block a few times and then suddenly change to a forehand attack. If the opponent does not hit strong forehand drives, push-block a series of fast shots to the opponent's forehand court.

Hit a few short balls to draw your opponent close

to the table, then hit deep and short shots alternately.

Hit underspins, then suddenly turn sideways and hit a forehand drive to your opponent's backhand court.

Countering an opponent who also uses the backhand push/forehand attack strategy

When you meet an opponent who uses the same tactics as you do, use speed and force in your push-block strokes, vary your placements with deep shots and shots to the corners of the table, or suddenly change to hitting underspin.

Try underspins to probe for an opening to attack.

If your opponent is slower afoot, hit the ball deep and short, to the left and right, to keep the opponent running.

If your opponent's reflexes are slower than yours, try to put more speed in your shots and try more deceptive maneuvers.

Counterattack Strategy

Hit a topspin to one side of the table and an attack stroke to the other, and vice versa.

Angle your spins to a corner of the table to move your opponent to that side, and then go for the other corner.

Hit fast spins to the corners and suddenly switch to a deep shot down the middle.

Hit deep topspins and low, short shots.

Hit short chops against underspins. The short

chops should be low, with spin, so your opponent cannot generate loopspin.

DOUBLE-ATTACK STRATEGY

The double attack is the most effective technique
in table tennis. Employing this tactic, one of our
players won the national championship four times
consecutively, and another player won three con-
secutive world championships. At one time, some
coaches thought the technique might be too difficult
to master for players of small stature. The feeling was
that smaller players might have trouble executing the
foot movements and the forehand attack. But that has
proven untrue. Players of small stature can utilize the
technique effectively if they hold the racket the horizontal way. Vertical racket holders at least 1.4 meters
(56 inches) tall can start with the backhand attack.
Intensive practice with a coach can overcome all diffi-
culties easily. But a player should

(a) Fully understand and execute the proper foot
    movements
(b) Learn how to control the racket with the fingers
    for the forehand and backhand strokes
(c) In practicing with a coach, concentrate on one
    technique at a time
(d) Coordinate finger control of the racket with foot
    movements and the backhand and forehand
    strokes

The double-attack strategy isn't simple to learn because the player must be well trained and adept at both the forehand and backhand techniques. Some players give up when they have difficulty executing the backhand strokes. But since this strategy is so effective in competition, it is well worth the training. Although the strategy is called double attack, the forehand drive plays a more important role, because almost everyone can exert a more powerful drive with the forehand than with the backhand.

Training routines

Stand behind the left side of the table so that the right side of your opponent's end, as you view it, is open to you. Also, if your opponent should launch an attack down the center of the table, you are in position to return the ball with your forehand.

Hold the racket in front of the right side of your chest, if you're a right-hander, and be prepared to meet an oncoming ball. Always return to this position after hitting. Many times, because of failure to return to this position, a player will lose control of the point.

Vertical racket holders should learn to combine the backhand attack with push-blocking, while horizontal racket holders should use fast-hit strokes. From observations in recent years, it seems apparent that the backhand loopspin attack and the hard-hit kill shot are not as effective as the backhand and forehand push-blocks.

Depending on where you stand, the double-attack tactics fall into two basic categories:

1. Close-to-the-table-fast-attack: The player stands about 30 cm to 40 cm from the table and the technique stresses speed, power and accurate placements.
2. Away-from-the-table-attack: The player stands about 50 cm to 60 cm from the table. Because the player is farther away, more power and accuracy in the strokes are required and the follow-through is more extended. The recent trend in attacking emphasizes speed.

Horizontal racket holders can combine loopspins with fast-hit attacking strokes. Some of the outstanding players from Yugoslavia and Hungary use these tactics.

Stance and foot movement

Stand behind the table, slightly left of the center, with the right foot slightly forward, if you are a right-hander, the left foot forward if you are a left-hander. The foot movements are mostly single-step. The movements should be quick and agile. Always return to the ready position after hitting. If your opponent's ball is short, use the two-step jump-over to meet the ball and return to the original position with the quick jump-over. Sometimes it's expedient to use the crossover step to reach the ball and then return to the original position with the quick jump-over.

	Backhand fast-hit attack, pull-spin and kill shots		
Stroke	Backhand fast-hit attack	Pull-spin	Kill shot
Getting ready	Stand about 30 cm from the table, right foot about half a foot in front of left foot, chest out, abdomen in.	Stand about 40 cm from table, right foot about ½ to 1 foot in front of left foot, body slightly bent. Stand slightly toward left. Horizontal racket holders should not turn as much to left.	Stand between 30 to 40 cm from the table, right foot about 6 inches forward of left foot.
	Arm positions: upper arm touches the right side of the chest, forearm points upward, angle between upper and forearm about 90°.	Arm positions: upper arm over chest, angle between upper arm and forearm over 90°.	Arm positions: upper arm over the right side of the chest, forearm and upper arm angle about 90°.
	Racket held in front of the left side of the chest, slightly tilted toward net.	Vertical racket holders hold the racket about waist high.	Racket is held over the left chest (lower than fast-hit), about same level

	Horizontal racket holders, near the abdomen. The racket is tilted back, or away from net.	with the peak of the bounce of the oncoming ball.
Contact the upper-middle part of the ball at the peak of ascent.	Contact the lower half of the ball at the peak of ascent or early stage of descent.	Contact the left-middle side of ball at the top of its bounce.
Hitting	Move the upper arm and forearm up from waist and whip down with force, pivoting at the waist. The wrist exerts force and controls the direction. The follow-through is a semicircle. The horizontal racket holder's follow-through is shorter, but needs more force from the wrist.	Start the upswing and exert force from forearm and upper arm in a forward-to-right direction. Smash down hard with all the force from the waist up through the arm.
Move forearm forward, exerting force, the wrist controlling the angle and direction. Meet the ball with a straightforward but rather short follow-through.		

	Backhand fast-hit attack, pull-spin and kill shots (cont.)
Some useful hints	1. Finger control of racket: *Vertical holders*: The forefinger should press on the front of the racket. The three fingers behind the racket control the angle of the racket. *Horizontal holders*: The thumb controls the angle of the racket.
	2. Elbow and wrist control of racket: Elbow pivoting controls the trajectory of your strokes. The wrist controls the "rub" of the in-close-to-the-table attack strokes.
	3. To execute the backhand attack strokes away from the table, you should exert force from the upper arm and forearm and coordinate the wrist maneuver in your follow-through. Horizontal racket holders should exert more wrist force than vertical racket holders. Contact middle-lower part of ball as it descends.

Service

Because you are positioned to the left of center, you are able to use both forehand and backhand serves. However, many players prefer the backhand serve, short to the opponent's right court, as you view the table, followed by a few topspins or underspins to the other side of the table. Besides the backhand serve, there are two basic forehand serves. One is the forehand service-placement where you stand behind the right court, if you are a right-hander, and after serving you move back to the center. The other is a forehand serve with spin, which should be struck from behind the left court and followed with attack strokes. Another option, less common, is the high serve with a lot of spin.

Returning service

With the exception of high-speed spins, which you should push-block back, you should meet the ball with force and begin developing an attack as quickly as possible. If the serve is short, gently rub or graze the ball at the peak of its bounce and drop it back on your opponent's side. For the underspin that comes in deep and low, counteract the spin with a pull and use loopspin. For the ball that bounces high, smash it with force.

DIAGRAM 38

Backhand attack

Backhand attack

After the player has perfected the basics of the forehand attack, push-blocking and rubbing, it's time to learn the backhand attack strokes (Diagram 38).

Close-to-the-table-fast-serve. This is favored by horizontal racket holders. The action is like push-blocking.

Fast-hit attacking. This is favored by vertical racket holders. Because it places a premium on speed, momentum and accuracy, this tactic is used to create opportunities for kill shots.

Pulling. This is a safe defensive technique, effective against underspins. It's designed to change the spin to your advantage. Because the ball speed is slow, this is not a direct point-winning tactic. However, it is useful for weathering an attack and to create an opportunity for your own attack.

Smashing. This is a point-winning shot. A sudden

smash catches an opponent off guard and has a significant psychological effect. Continue smashing even if your opponent returns the ball to your backhand court.

Backhand attack pointers. At the outset, learn the correct stance, foot movements and body control.

The hand and foot movements and the control of the racket with your fingers and wrist need to be coordinated. Develop the habit of moving your feet before your hands. If you move your feet to the proper position to meet an oncoming ball, you'll be prepared to make the stroke without overextending your arm or losing your balance.

Combine the forehand and backhand attack tactics in training and give equal attention to both.

In competition, don't be reluctant to use the backhand attack when the ball comes to your backhand court.

Practice with a coach. A coach's interest generally produces a higher standard of play. Younger players who train only with their peers tend to lose the incentive to improve at times.

Intensive training routines

Practice serving the ball to designated points, and then try deep placements.

Return the service to designated points, hitting diagonal placements, straight shots, then deep shots. Emphasize wide-angle shots in the diagonal placements and speed in the straight shots.

Practice returning topspins, underspins and then random spins. Start by returning the topspins with push-blocks, then try the forehand attack standing sideways, next the backhand attack, and finally kill shots. Return the underspins by rubbing or grazing, then chopping and smashing. Gradually increase the degree of your spins and lower the trajectory of your shots.

Start with warm-up exercises for both the forehand and backhand, then more exercises for the backhand than the forehand, and finally mix the exercises at random. At the outset, restrict the sphere of action to half of the table, and gradually expand to the full table. Stress speed and direction in the backhand attack, and force and the angle of attack in the forehand attack.

Other training procedures

Develop two kinds of diagonal serve, one to the center of your opponent's court, the other to the corner (Diagram 39).

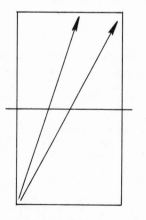

Diagram 39

Diagonal serve

Practice your backhand attack technique against an opponent's backhand push/forehand attack tactics.

Have a coach or partner hit the ball to your backhand court and practice rubbing or grazing the ball to set up a forceful attacking shot.

Practice the backhand-attack-combined-with-forehand-attack while standing sideways with a player who push-blocks.

Practice push-blocking with a coach or partner who hits once to your backhand, once to your forehand.

Hit a succession of backhand attack strokes and a forehand attack stroke against a push-blocker.

Pointers

Because of the grip they use, horizontal racket holders are better able to use the backhand to serve, attack, hit loop strokes or impart spins. There are also tactics that are especially suitable for horizontal racket holders—for instance, against a hard smash, the fast-hit technique is effective to regain the initiative. Against loopspin, the horizontal racket holder can lob. Also, the backhand loop is effective against underspin if you follow up with attacking strokes.

Practice with a chopper. Besides learning how to return chops with your forehand, you'll also learn how to deal with wide-angle shots that land in the corner of your backhand court—the tactic of floating the ball back. To deal with heavy chops to your backhand court, counterloop with your backhand before establishing position to initiate a forehand attack.

The horizontal racket holder who uses a pips-in racket and wants to develop the double-attack strategy should learn how to hit forehand and backhand loopspins. First concentrate on placements. Next practice loopdrives against a chopper. After you have mastered the technique of loopspins and loopdrives, combine both in your practice.

Strategy against the backhand push/ forehand attack

Let's consider the advantages and disadvantages for the opponent who uses the backhand push/forehand attack against you. The style affords the opponent good control for balls that you hit short, which the opponent can easily return to set up a counterattack. The disadvantages are that the opponent usually stands behind the backhand court for defense, leaving an open space in the forehand court and also leaving the opponent in poor position for balls that come in fast and deep. When forced to move back, the opponent yields positional advantage for fast-hitting and push-blocking. So the strategy you should use is as follows:

Remember that the opponent's weak side is the forehand court. Hit a few fast topspins or underspins to the far corner of the opponent's backhand court, forcing the opponent to move farther away from the forehand court and leaving a wide-open space for you to hit a kill shot into the forehand court. Besides fastspin shots to the opponent's backhand court, hit a few short balls up the middle or to the opponent's forehand court. This moves your opponent around and can make the opponent psychologically insecure.

Serve wide-angle fast-spins to the two corners of the table and then hit deep shots down the middle. Increase the speed of your shots and look for an opening for a kill shot.

When under attack down the center, to regain the initiative, if you're a right-hander, move to your left a little and counterattack with placements to the opponent's forehand court, or defend with forehand push-blocking until you get an opportunity to launch a backhand attack. The horizontal racket holder can chop or short-chop to upset the opponent's tactics.

Strategy against the double attack

Generally the center offers the best potential for attacking. Start there and probe for a weak point, left and right, front and back.

Alter the direction of the balls the opponent hits to you. For example, if the opponent serves cross-court, return the ball straight across the table. Accelerate the speed of your shots.

Try short chops if your topspins do not produce results, and if that doesn't work, switch to underspins.

Against the counterchop in the center:

Hit fast-spins to the left side of the table, as you see it, and smashes or chops to the right side.

Hit fast-spins down the center followed by chops to either the left or right side of the table.

Hit fast-spins to the corners, followed by either a
short or deep shot.

Combine spins with chops or short chops. This tactic
is especially effective against an opponent who is
not a strong attacker.

Pointers. Horizontal racket holders, because of
their grip, are able to apply more power to the backhand loopspin serve and the loopdrive.

Young players should practice the chop as a tactic
against an attacker using loopspins. The chop can
help you to ride out the crisis—until an opening to
counterattack develops.

LOOPSPINS AND LOOPDRIVES

Loopspins and loopspin drives are accelerated topspins. Loopspins are slower than loopdrives but have
heavier spins. Loopdrives also have a lower trajectory.
Both are new techniques rooted in the development
of the pips-in racket. Since the Japanese stunned the
world of table tennis with loopspins and loopdrives
in 1960, players from different countries have re-
fined the technique and developed their own innovations off the basic strokes. The shots of the Chinese
players, for example, are different from those of the
Europeans and Japanese. Our loops are executed
close to the table, designed to generate more power
and speed and to be more deceptive. At international
competitions, the loopserves and loopdrives of our

players often produced points within the first three strokes. The shots were so fast and carried such forward momentum they were nearly impossible to return. You can imagine the psychological effects on our opponents. Even when the loops don't lead to a point immediately, they force the opponent into a defensive position.

Although the loopspins and loopdrives are not easy skills to acquire, they are so valuable that young players simply need to be determined to work hard to master the techniques. The key qualities of an effective loopspin or loopdrive are speed, heavy spin, deceptive placement and an aggressive force in the stroke. In training, the player should learn to combine loops with the forehand fast serve and the forehand close-to-the-table techniques on the attack.

For defense, the player should combine push-blocking with backhand counterattack techniques. In addition, the player should learn the close-to-the-table and away-from-the-table exchange of spins and counterattack techniques.

In brief, there are two kinds of loop: (1) the loopdrive, characterized by high speed and forward momentum, with a lower trajectory than a loopspin, (2) the loopspin, characterized by heavy topspin but less speed than the loopdrive. Whether you use a pips-in or pips-out racket makes a difference in the spin and speed of your loops.

Stance and technique for hitting loopspins and loopdrives (using the pips-in racket)

	Loopspin (Diagram 40)	Loopdrive (Diagram 41)
The stance	About 40 cm from table, left foot slightly forward, knees bent, body bent slightly forward, weight on right foot, body angle with table about 40°.	Basically the same as loopspin, but weight on both feet.
Arm and racket position	Arm is stretched out, hanging down naturally, holding racket tilted a little bit forward.	Upper arm is stretched out a little more than for loopspin.
When to meet ball	Middle of ball as it descends.	Upper-middle of ball at peak of ascent.
Stroke and follow-through	Swing forearm forward, accelerated with force from the upper arm to meet the ball in an upswing, pivoting at the waist. Follow-through ends with racket near the face, body weight on both feet.	Swing the whole arm with force from the body and arm, pivoting at the waist, to whip forward in a low trajectory arc. After follow-through, racket is about 30 cm in front of the neck, body weight is on the left foot.

1   2   3

DIAGRAM 40

Loopspin

1   2   3

DIAGRAM 41

Loopdrive

Slow loop (using pips-out racket)

Basically, the technique is the same for the pips-out or pips-in racket holder. But the pips-out racket does not stick to the ball like the pips-in racket and does not generate as much spin as the pips-in racket. So the player should use a little wrist movement to extend contact and produce more spin. The follow-through also is shorter, employing force from the forearm, and the trajectory is lower than with the pips-in racket.

Sidespin loop

At contact with the ball, a slight rub to the left or right with your racket angled forward or backward imparts sidespin as you push forward.

Nonspin loop

Hold your racket tilted slightly backward. Contact the middle-lower part of the ball. Do not rub. Just push forward and upward.

Backhand loop (for the horizontal racket holder)

The basics for loopspin for the horizontal racket holder are the same as for the vertical racket holder. Because of the variations in the grip, however, the horizontal racket holder can execute a backhand loopspin more effectively than the vertical racket holder.

The player should stand about 40 cm behind the
table in a crouch, body weight on both feet to enable
the player to exert force from the waist up through
the arm and to shift the weight to the soles of the
feet without loss of balance. The racket is tilted toward the net. Aim to strike the upper-middle part of
the ball when the racket, for right-handers, is in front
of the left side of the chest. For the stroke, move the
forearm and upper arm forward in an upswing with
force. At the moment the racket rubs the ball, accelerate with the wrist. Follow through and finish
with your racket in front of the right side of your
face (Diagram 42).

DIAGRAM 42

Backhand loopspin

Backhand loopspin is not as powerful as forehand
loopspin. Most often, backhand loopspin is used to
return serve or ride out an attack. To employ it effectively, the horizontal racket holder needs a little
more wrist force than the vertical racket holder.

Training

Foot movement: Because the sphere of action for

loops covers most of the end of the table, developing agility is important. The quick jump-over is most often associated with the stroke because it can be executed to either side expediently, and the player can also use the quick jump-over to return to the ready position after making the stroke.

Placement practice: Practice placements to designated points until you develop good control; then combine the hand and foot movement exercises with your placements.

Intensive practice: Have a coach or partner hit (1) underspins, (2) push-blocks to your forehand and backhand courts, (3) shots for you to return while standing sideways, (4) diagonal shots, (5) straight shots to set up loopspins and loopdrives by you.

Practice with a chopper: Practice (1) diagonal shots, (2) straight shots, (3) mixing both at random.

Practice with a push-blocker: Practice (1) diagonal shots, (2) straight shots for you to loop while standing sideways, (3) placements to your forehand and backhand for you to counterloop to one spot.

Pointers

In working on loops, a player should also learn to combine them with kill shots. Because loopspin is generally executed farther from the table than the close-to-the-table-fast-hit technique, the opponent tends to return the ball with gentle blocking. Such returns give you an opportunity to hit your shots forcefully and follow with a chop or kill shot.

The secret of a good looper is the ability, at the split second when the racket contacts the ball, to rub with speed and force. The angle or tilt of the racket has a significant influence on the result. To produce heavy topspin, the racket generally should be held straight or perpendicular. The ball should be contacted with a steady pull-up motion, never a shaky downward motion.

The loop is not a fast-hit shot. Because the player stands away from the table, the loop is executed with force from the waist up.

In the correct stance, the left foot is, for a right-hander, a little forward of the right foot.

At the moment of contact, the body weight shifts to the left foot from the right foot. This shift enables the player to generate force from the waist up.

To add force to the backhand loop, the horizontal racket holder should squat for balance.

The follow-through for the loop is more extensive than the follow-through for most attack strokes. So the player should make extra certain of getting the arm back to the ready position after making the stroke.

Before practicing the loop shots, undertake a daily program of body conditioning exercises to strengthen the muscles of the arms, shoulders and waist to prevent injuries and muscle pulls.

Combine the loops with fast-hit strokes.

Against a fast-hit attacker, serve a short underspin and follow with loopspins. If your opponent serves a fast-hit topspin, use the backhand push-block to apply pressure to the left corner of your opponent's side of the table, as you view it, and continue with forehand attacks while standing sideways.

If your right side is under attack, use loopspins to create an opening for a fast-hit attack. If your left side is under attack, counterloop or use backhand attack strokes, making sure you return to the ready position after each stroke.

Try launching a series of spins to your opponent's forehand court, using your forehand and standing behind the center of the table. You can use a forehand loopdrive to your advantage against your opponent's forehand attack strokes.

Serve low underspins to your opponent's backhand corner, following with a short shot to your opponent's forehand court. If your opponent returns with a short chop, try a few loopspins. If your opponent returns the serve with loopspin, counter with a loopdrive. Apply force to your diagonal shots and speed to your straight shots.

Serve deep down the center of the table with heavy spins, or without spin, or try the high serve with either topspin, underspin or sidespin.

Counter a loopspin serve with a loopspin and follow with a loopdrive attack.

Against a defensive player, loops are especially effective. Combine loopspins and loopdives by (1) hitting loopspins to both corners and then a kill shot down the center, (2) hitting a loopspin down the center and following with smash shots to either corner, (3) hitting a short loopspin just over the net and following with a kill shot or a loopdrive.

Refining your technique

Work on accelerating the spins in your loopspins and the power in your loopdrives.

Learn how to hit loopspins and non-spin loops with the same follow-through so your opponents will have difficulty distinguishing one from the other.

In practicing loopspins and sidespin loops, intersperse the drills with placements and pushblocks.

For the horizontal racket holder: combine backhand loops with a kill shot or a short chop.

While standing behind the center of the table, practice exchanging loopspins and loopdrives. Learn how to counteract the momentum of a loopdrive by holding your racket tilted forward and simultaneously exerting force in your pull-up and forward motion.

Combine a backhand loop attack with wide-angled loop placements to the table corners. To shift to a forehand loopdrive, use the two-step crossover to get back into position, moving the right foot first if you are a right-hander. The horizontal racket holder can use the quick jump-over to get into position for a backhand loop attack.

COMBINING CHOPS AND
ATTACK STROKES

The chop is an underspin produced by a slice-down action on the ball. In international competition, our players have used the chop as an effective defensive technique combined with attack tactics. With its unpredictable spins, the chop has a place in the strategy of both defense and attacking. Basically, there are two kinds of chop tactics:

1. *Chops combined with counterattacking.* This tactic stresses more the chop techniques and follows with attack strokes. The chop is not only a defensive technique against topspins, but also a stroke that can lead to counterattacking and winning a point. A good chopper can deliver the stroke with or without spin to confuse an opponent, then suddenly unleash a kill shot.

2. *Attack shots combined with chops.* This tactic stresses more the attack technique, blending in the chop for defense. It is a formidable combination. Many world-class players employ this style, using it effectively to defend and regain control of the table.

Position

For defense and to gain a positional advantage leading to a counterattack, the best position for a chopper is to stand about 120 cm behind the table.

Forehand chops

Forehand diagonal chop: Chop with force from your forehand and wrist. The slice-down action between your racket and the ball generates the friction that produces the heavy spin in a chop. Even more force from the upper arm is needed when you are far from the table. Contact the lower-middle part of the ball. If you're a right-hander, your racket should be angled diagonally at the opponent's forehand court and moved downward and forward. Make sure to return to the ready position after the stroke.

Forehand straight-line chop: The technique is the same as for the diagonal chop except that the racket is held head down and aimed straight across the table.

Backhand chops

Backhand diagonal chop: The basic technique is the same as for the forehand, except that the shot should be aimed toward the opponent's backhand court.

Backhand straight-line chop: Again, the technique is the same, except the shot should be aimed toward the opponent's forehand court.

Pointers for chops

In setting the angle between the racket and the ball, the smaller the point of contact, the heavier the spin that will be imparted to the ball.

The racket should be held flat, almost parallel to

the floor, because for most chops you need to meet the ball as it descends, contacting the lower-middle part of the ball.

At the moment of contact, exert force and slice down to accelerate the spin. For a non-spin chop, contact the ball with more force and less rubbing action.

To chop a high ball, hold your racket straight and contact the middle part of the ball. Chop hard downward and forward.

To chop a ball as it descends, hold the racket tilted back and contact the lower-middle part of the ball. Chop downward and forward.

To chop a ball lower than the table, hold your racket tilted back to almost flat. Contact the bottom of the ball. Chop extremely hard and push upward and forward.

To chop a hard-hit ball, hold your racket flat to absorb the impact and neutralize the action.

Training for chops

Have a partner hit forehand spins to your left or right, first to designated spots and then at random. Practice exchanging chops and spins leading to a kill shot. Watch your opponent's stroke carefully to determine the spin and force of an oncoming ball. At the same time, work on foot movements and get back to the ready position after every stroke.

Have a partner serve straight-line spins to your forehand and backhand courts for you to chop diagonally.

Have a partner hit attack strokes diagonally to your forehand and backhand courts for you to hit straight chops.

Have a partner hit topspins to different parts of the table. Return them accordingly.

Have a partner hit deep shots down the middle of the table for you to chop to the two corners. If the shot is a forehand, return it with a forehand chop. If your partner executes the shot while standing sideways, return it with a backhand chop.

Have a partner serve topspins, then suddenly hit a short shot followed by a fast-hit deep shot. You'll need to move forward quickly to reach the short shot and move back quickly to reach the deep shot. If you cannot get back fast enough, try blocking or a chop close to the table.

The chop is the most effective tactic against heavy loopspins or loopdrives. With the advances in technique in recent years, many kinds of loops have been invented by table tennis players around the world. And with the innovations, schools of counterstrategy have developed. A well-trained chopper need not fear loops if the chopper is confident and skilled in the technique of slowing down heavy loopspin and making it work to his advantage.

To chop against a heavy topspin loop: Hold your racket straight, head down, handle up, and slice down, making contact at the lower-middle part of the ball. Exert a force appropriate to the degree of spin on the oncoming ball. But don't push forward too hard because excessive forward motion will send the ball out of play.

To chop against a loopdrive: Loopdrives have more speed but less topspin and less arc than loopspins. The basics to deal with them are the same as for countering loopspins except that you should use more force and more forward motion.

To chop against heavy and weak sidespins: Contact the ball on either side, angling your racket toward the direction you want the shot to take. Fast foot movement is critical to the success of your return.

Strategy for chops

Because there is a vast difference between the stance for chopping and for attacking, when you want to shift you'll need to adjust quickly. Usually you can make one step or a half-step to execute the attack shot. But the action must be fast and decisive if you want to gain the initiative. Before you counter-attack, you should try a few deceptive chops to catch your opponent off guard.

Training routines for attack

Practice in a group of three: one serves, one loops, and one chops.

Practice with a looper. Have the partner hit loop-spins and loopdrives to you so you can practice fore-hand and backhand chops, working on control of low-trajectory shots and counterattack tactics such as away-from-the-table spins and sudden short chops.

Vertical racket holders should practice push-blocking and use backhand wrist snap for high balls. Also, try the forehand racket switch. Pretend to hit with a forehand to one side of your opponent's court and with a sudden wrist movement switch and hit the ball to the other side of the table with a backhand (Diagram 43).

DIAGRAM 43

Forehand racket switch

Pointers for attack

For an attack combined with chops, it is advantageous for the player to have a racket with pips-out rubber on one side and pips-in rubber on the other, especially against heavy loopspins.

Try a succession of spins and placements to attack, using the chop for defense.

Try a sudden attack of short chops, keeping the ball low to take the initiative.

Combine short chops and chops with the forehand and backhand attack technique to launch an attack after returning serve.

Chop deep and short.

Counterattack by forcing your opponent to one corner to create an opening for finesse shots.

Try blocking and chopping combined—a chop with a surprise block or chop and a light block followed by a sudden change of spin.

Against an opponent who stands far back, hit short chops. Against an opponent who is slow, hit deep shots and wide-angle shots to the corners of the table.

Use chops followed by loopspins to set up a counterattack.

Against an opponent whose style is attacking combined with chopping, follow the basics of the double-attack strategy. Against an opponent whose style is chopping combined with counterattacking, try a few deceptive spins and follow with attacking strokes.

Basic Guidelines for Chopping

Chop	Stroke	Meeting the ball		Foot Movement
		Point of contact	Timing	
Forehand/backhand close-to-the-table chops	Use a short follow-through, with forearm force; slice downward and forward.	Middle-to-lower part of the ball	At peak of ascent or at early stage of descent.	Single-step, quick jump-over and two-step jump-over.
Forehand/backhand far-from-the-table chops	Exert force with the forearm and upper arm and chop downward.	Middle-to-lower part of the ball	Almost at the end of descent. Contact the ball earlier if you are closer to the table.	Same as above, plus the crossover step.
Chop down the middle of table	With a fast and decisive movement, chop down and forward.	Middle-to-lower part of the ball	Same as above.	Quick jump-over to one side.

Basic Guidelines for Chopping

Chop	Stroke	Meeting the ball		Foot Movement
		Point of contact	Timing	
Returning a surprise attack shot	If a shot is short, hold the racket over the ball and chop down and forward. If the shot is deep, exert force from the forearm and upper arm, chop hard down and forward. Estimate the force of the shot and determine how hard to chop.	Middle-to-lower part of the ball	Depending on how close you are to the table: the closer you are, the sooner you make contact.	Single-step and quick jump-over.
Returning short shots	Stretch the arm toward the ball, slice and rub downward with a wrist snap.	Lower part of the ball	Early stage of descent.	One big single step forward and a crossover step.

How to Execute the Various Chops

1. *Forehand and backhand chops*

   Forehand chops: Move the upper arm back and swing forward and downward.

   Backhand chop: Use less upper arm movement and a shorter stroke, but apply forearm and wrist force.

2. *With spin or without spin*

   With spin: Contact the lower-middle part of the ball. Slice and rub downward to accelerate the spin.

   No spin: Contact the lower-middle part of the ball. Chop with more forward force and with only slight rub.

3. *Diagonal or straight*

   Diagonal: Hit the lower-middle part of the ball and angle the racket to right or left with a down and forward stroke.

   Straight: Hit the lower-middle part of the ball with a downward and forward stroke.

4. *Vertical versus horizontal racket holder*

   To chop, the vertical racket holder must have agile foot movements, exert more force from the upper arm and use a longer follow-through than the horizontal racket holder. When returning wide-angle shots and hard-hit shots, more pivoting from the waist to exert force is also necessary for the vertical racket holder.

5. *Angling of racket*

   To chop a high ball, hold the racket head straight up, hit the middle part of ball and chop down hard. To chop a ball as it descends, tilt the racket back slightly, contact the lower-middle part of the ball, slice down and forward.

To chop a ball that is lower than the table, tilt the racket back to almost flat, slice the bottom of the ball and push forward.

To chop a hard-hit ball, hold the racket flat (to reduce pressure on the racket) and push forward hard to counteract the impact.

SERVING AND RETURNING SERVE

Serving is a direct point-winning technique. In recent years, many new serves have been developed for international championships. The objective is to be fast, accurate and deceptive. Often, a subtle, hard-to-detect movement of the wrist can produce significant variations in the character of the flight of the ball. Following are the various kinds of serve.

Fast-hit serves are based on high speed and placement, designed to surprise the opponent. They are fast-hit to the end of the table, either to the corners or down the center.

Forehand fast-hit serve

Stand with the left foot forward, if you're a right-hander, and the body turned sideways to the right. The ball is held in the palm of the left hand, the right forearm hangs naturally, the elbow up slightly. The racket-holding hand is about 20 cm behind the other hand. After tossing the ball, swing the racket arm back and forward to make contact when the ball is about 15 cm from the table, hitting the right-upper part of the ball (Diagram 44).

DIAGRAM 44

Forehand fast-hit serve

Backhand fast-hit serve

Stand with the right foot forward, if you're a right-hander, body turned to the left, the ball in the palm of the left hand held in front of the left side of the abdomen. The right arm holding the racket, with the elbow bent, is over the left hand. Toss the ball, and when it is about 20 cm to 25 cm from the table, hit the ball with the racket tilted back, exerting force with the forearm. Whip the racket swiftly toward the right, contacting the upper-middle part of the ball. The wrist determines the direction. The follow-through is completed when the racket is high over the right shoulder (Diagram 45).

DIAGRAM 45

Backhand fast-hit underspin serve

108

Backhand fast-hit underspin serve

The stance and the stroke are the same as for the backhand fast-hit serve, except that at contact the thumb presses down hard on the racket to exert more force and the racket slices the lower-middle part of the ball to impart underspin (Diagrams 46 and 47).

DIAGRAM 46

Backhand fast-hit underspin serve

DIAGRAM 47

Arm movement and racket tilt

Short serve

The purpose of the short serve is to lure your opponent close to the table, creating openings for attack shots. The stance is the same as for fast-hit serves, but the short serve should be short and low. The racket is tilted back, and at contact the forearm and wrist apply only slight force (Diagram 48).

DIAGRAM 48

Short serve

The short serve may be struck either forehand or backhand and should be interspersed among fast-hit serves. Most beginners start with the forehand but more experienced players prefer the backhand. By angling the racket at contact with the ball, you can serve either fast-hit or short style as part of the double-attack strategy.

Usually, the right-handed player stands behind his or her left side of the table to serve the backhand fast-hit topspin or underspin, then follows with a short shot and an attack shot. Against an opponent who uses the chop counterattack, you can serve the backhand fast-hit serve to either the left, middle or right side, and follow with a short shot to draw the opponent forward and create an opening for a deep attack.

Spin serves

There are three basic spin serves: (1) forehand topspin or underspin to the left side of the table, (2) backhand topspin or underspin to the right side, (3) spins or nonspins. Their advantage is that the difference in technique to produce the various spins is subtle and can be masked effectively to fool your opponent. The stance is the same as the basic stance for the forehand and backhand fast-hit serves. Sometimes, to use the forehand topspin or underspin to initiate the backhand push/forehand attack strategy, the right-handed player can stand behind his own backhand court and serve backhand to the opponent's backhand. This puts a right-handed player on the left side, in a natural position to hit forehand on over-the-table return. This is advantageous to the player who plans to use forehand attacks after the opponent returns the serve.

Forehand serves to the left side of the table

Topspin. Right-handers should stand with the left foot forward, the body turned slightly toward the right, the ball in the palm of the left hand, which is in front of the right side of the abdomen. Toss the ball and extend your right arm in an upswing exerting force with the forearm and wrist (Diagram 49). Swing forcefully toward the ball, at the same time pressing down hard on the racket with the forefinger while the three fingers behind the racket relax. At contact, rub the middle-to-left part of the ball (Diagram 50). If you want to short-serve, tilt your racket forward a little. The ball should bounce at midtable on your side and land near the net on the opponent's side.

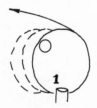

DIAGRAM 49

Forehand topspin serve

DIAGRAM 50

Forehand topspin serve, as racket contacts ball

Underspin. The stance is the same as for topspin but the stroke, of course, differs (Diagram 51). At contact, press the racket back with the thumb and rub downward on the middle-left part of the ball (Diagram 52).

DIAGRAM 51

Forehand underspin serve

DIAGRAM 52

Forehand underspin serve,
as racket contacts ball

Backhand serve

Topspin. Right-handers should stand behind the left side of the table, right foot forward, body turned to the left, the ball in the palm of the left hand, which is in front of the left side of the abdomen. The right forearm is behind and lower than the left hand. The racket head is held up, toward the left shoulder, the arm stretched out slightly. When the ball is about net high, swing down firmly, exerting force with the forearm and wrist (Diagram 53). At contact press down on the racket with the forefinger and rub the middle-right part of the ball. For a wide-angle shot, rub more to the left. For a short serve, hold the racket a little straighter.

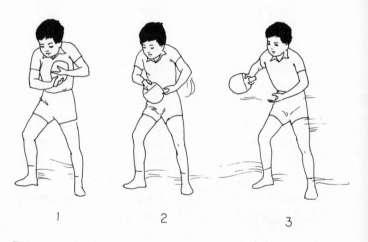

1   2   3

Diagram 53

Backhand topspin serve

Underspin. The stroke is similar to the stroke for the topspin except that, at contact, tilt the racket back with the thumb and rub the middle-right part of the ball (Diagram 54).

1   2   3

DIAGRAM 54

Backhand underspin serve

Forehand spin serve

If you're a right-hander, stand behind the table just left of the center line, the left foot forward, the body turned slightly to the right. The left hand is in front of the abdomen; the right hand, with the elbow slightly bent, is by the right side of the body. Toss the ball and move the forearm in an upswing, whipping forward toward the ball. Contact the ball when it is about net high, pressing down on the racket with the thumb to tilt the racket back and slice the lower-middle part of the ball (Diagram 55).

Forehand nonspin serve

The technique is the same as for the spin serve, except that contact is made with reduced force (Diagram 56).

DIAGRAM 55

Spin serve

DIAGRAM 56

Nonspin serve

Backhand spin and nonspin serves

The techniques are the same as for the forehand, except the direction is reversed. These serves are commonly used with loop tactics and the backhand push/forehand attack strategy.

Flick spin serves

The flick is a deceptive motion to confuse your opponent. Sometimes the flick will cause the ball to float or to fluctuate. The key elements of the technique are a high ball toss and a fast wrist flick, producing a short serve with a low trajectory.

The setup is the same as for the topspin and underspin serves. But at contact, the wrist suddenly imparts spin and direction to the ball, moving left or right, up or down. A deceptive flick can be made either after contact (Diagram 57) or before contact (Diagram 58). In either case, the intent is to make it appear as if you are serving in a certain direction that you aren't.

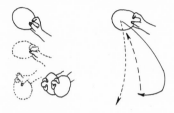

DIAGRAM 57

Flick after contact

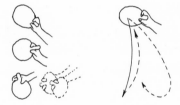

DIAGRAM 58

Flick before contact

High serve

This is a spectacular maneuver, executed by tossing the ball at least six to seven feet high in preparation for the serve. The gravitational force of the falling ball and the speed of your racket accelerate the speed and spin of the serve and add a psychological element. The spin and direction you impart to the ball are concealed until the last moment. For the right-hander, the stance has the body turned to the right, left foot forward, with the player in a semi-crouching position (Diagram 59). The right hand, with the racket handle pointing down, is high over the right shoulder. As the ball falls, if you make contact with a left-to-right upward rub, you generate topspin. If you make contact with a left-to-right, slicing-down action, underspin is produced.

DIAGRAM 59

Crouch for the high serve

Training routines

Serve forehand and backhand to various partners, using different spins.

Practice one or two sets of serves with one partner and a different set of serves with another partner. A set means combining a few serves with different spins and placements. For example, you can serve a few forehand topspin or backspin serves combined with some straight-line fast-hit serves. Or you may serve a few backhand fast-hit topspins and backspins combined with a short serve. The idea is to mix the serves so you don't serve to your opponent's strengths.

After perfecting the serving techniques, some time should be devoted to tactics and strategies, utilizing the serves to initiate an attack. For example, after serving a forehand underspin to an opponent's backhand court, if the opponent uses the backhand push/ forehand attack strategy, you are probably going to get a backhand push to your backhand court, and you can anticipate such a maneuver. If the opponent is another type of attacker, the serve would probably be returned in another way. To combine your serve with an attack, you should have a succession of shots planned and some strategy in mind.

Returning serve

Returning serve is just as important as serving. The most common causes of failure are tenseness, poor judgment, slow reflexes, improper foot movement and standing too far from the table. Therefore players should:

Keep calm.

Stand in the proper place. Watch your opponent's serving motion and adjust accordingly. For example, if your opponent stands behind his or her forehand court, you can anticipate wide-angle shots to your forehand court and you should prepare by moving closer to your forehand court. If your opponent appears ready to serve to your backhand court, move over to that side of the table.

Study your opponent's strokes and how he makes contact with the ball to determine the character of the serve and the direction it is headed.

Aim your returns to your opponent's weak side and to parts of the table that extend his reach.

Use all kinds of techniques and be unpredictable.

INTENSIVE TRAINING

THE STANDARD OF TABLE TENNIS IS RISING CONTIN-
ually. New techniques are developed for competition
and, with them, new training methods. In the 1960s,
intensive training became popular. Players in Sweden, Romania, Yugoslavia and Japan began using
ball machines for practice. More recently, a machine
capable of delivering 90 balls a minute has been
developed and is in use in Japan and Europe. One of
the remarkable features of the innovation is that the
balls are collected in a net and may be fed back to
the player indefinitely.

Advantages of intensive training

By the machine's serving the same type of shot to a fixed point repeatedly, the player can acquire the technique to deal with that shot more quickly. The machines serve up balls at least 50 percent faster than another human.

The intensive work also helps players to coordinate their movements and develop control of the table, refining not only tactics but speed, reflexes and agility.

Of special value is training to develop the player's foot movements. The player learns to move his or her feet spontaneously to a position to hit the ball effectively.

Intensive drills also serve to build up a player's physical stamina, although conditioning should be achieved in large part through daily physical exercise.

Statistics of the player's performance can be compiled so progress can be measured and more attention directed to weak areas.

A training aid

A wooden box that is easy to construct may be used to advantage to store balls conveniently for intensive training (Diagram 60). The box should be a little lower than the table. It serves as a collection point for balls and minimizes disruptions to other players.

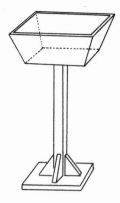

DIAGRAM 60

Box to store balls

Practicing serves

Assemble three or four players to practice together, taking turns in serving and hitting various types of shots. The players should study each other's form carefully and not be reticent about offering advice.

Serve to the corners of the table.

At the outset, the server should allow the balls to bounce first. Later, the server should serve without bouncing the balls first.

Intensive practice for two players

Each player assembles 20 to 30 balls and serves and receives alternately, without stopping, hitting forehand and backhand attack shots, kill shots and other kinds of strokes. The players should be of comparable ability.

Pointers

Don't serve too quickly at the beginning. Speed is not important at this stage. Learning the proper technique is more important. Speed may be increased later.

Stress quality not quantity. Practice just enough to promote interest and further technique, but not so much as to become utterly fatigued. Generally, a player should hit no more than 200 balls in any exercise.

Proceed slowly enough to ensure that the hand, body and foot movements are all correct and coordinated. Slow down if a player appears to be becoming shaky.

Intensive training should be systematic and regular.

DOUBLES

Half of the categories in international table tennis tournaments are doubles. A player should, of course, start with the basics for singles. But later doubles will add an enjoyable dimension to the game. The players should complement each other's talents and work out a strategy that will blend their skills most effectively.

CHOOSING PARTNERS

The two players should not only follow the same strategy but should be able to work compatibly, so that they do not get in each other's way and are able to execute their strokes without hindrance.

Best combinations

A backhand push/forehand attacker paired with a looper or a double-attacker. They stand at different positions at the end of the table, one in front, one in back.

A backhand attacker paired with a forehand attacker. One player stands behind the forehand court, the other behind the backhand court.

A short-chopper paired with a far-from-the-table chopper. This combination works well for counter-attacking. The short-chopper stands close to the table in position to hit placement shots to the corners or kill shots. The chopper stands back to hit spins or attack shots.

. . . Less desirable combinations

Two backhand push/forehand attackers or two double-attackers. Because both pairs stand at the same depth behind the table, they are prone to getting in each other's way. They also leave one side of the table and the middle vulnerable to attack.

Two choppers at the back or two choppers in front. The former combination invites opponents to hit short chops or drop shots, the latter deep spins and drives. Both are disastrous. The players are also likely to encumber each other.

Worst combinations

A close-to-the-table attacker paired with a short-chopper or a far-from-the-table attacker paired with a far-from-the-table chopper. These combinations make it virtually impossible to hit a succession of attacking shots or for the chopper to defend effectively. The players will get in each other's paths nearly all the time.

TECHNIQUE AND STRATEGY

Following are some of the more effective movement patterns for doubles:

Diagonally—player A moves to the left and player B moves to the right (Diagram 61).

Small half-circle—this pattern is commonly used by a backhand push/forehand attack combination when there isn't time to move back to deal with a wide-angle shot (Diagram 62).

Forward and backward—far-from-the-table choppers or attackers use this pattern (Diagram 63).

Horizontal loops—this pattern is actually formed by two small-circle steps. Choppers like to employ this pattern to deal with wide-angle diagonal shots (Diagram 64).

DIAGRAM 61

Diagonal pattern

DIAGRAM 62

Small half-circle

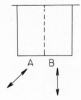

DIAGRAM 63

Forward and backward

DIAGRAM 64

Horizontal loops

TACTICS

Remember to get out of your partner's way immediately after you hit the ball.

Against opponents who use placement tactics:

1. Counterattack with placement shots followed by deep shots.
2. Return deep, then look for an opening for a kill shot.
3. Aim a succession of attack shots to a corner, then suddenly switch your attention to another spot.

Against opponents who are backhand push/forehand attackers and usually stand slightly to their left: try a few wide-angle shots to the corners or a succession of short shots to the right court, as you view the table.

Against two choppers, one in front, one in back:

1. Hit a few shots down the center followed by deep shots to the two corners.
2. Hit short placements to the side where the chopper is in back and deep shots to the side where the chopper stands in front.

Serve to set up an attack

In doubles, your opponent's return of your serve is to be hit by your partner. To follow your serve with an attack, the strong and weak points of the opposition should be considered. For example, if the opponent receiving your serve is a forehand attacker, serve short. If the opponent stands to his or her right, serve a heavy spin or a short serve to the center. If the opponent is a looper, serve low and short. If the opponent is a close-to-the-table attacker, serve heavy spins or try a non-spin serve to confuse the opponent and create an opening for your partner to initiate an attack.

Returning service to set up an attack

Returning service in doubles lends itself to initiating an attack. The type of attack should be determined by where your partner is standing and where the server's partner is standing. Also take into consideration the opposition's weaknesses and strengths as well as yours and your partner's. For example, if the server's partner stands facing left, attack the right side. If the partner runs to the right, attack with straight fast-hits. If the partner stands back, hit side-spins to the side edges of the table. If the partner stands close to the table, use fast-hit deep shots. If your partner is a forehand attacker, hit wide-angle diagonal shots to your opponents. If your partner is strong on backhand attacking, hit to your opponents' backhand court so your partner can exploit his or her specialty.

How to determine which partner should receive the serve

For purposes of explanation, we will designate A and B as partners receiving the service and C and D as partners on the serving side.

If A is a stronger player than B, and C is a better attacker than D, then A should receive D's serve to control C's attack, while B initiates an attack on D.

In mixed doubles, set yourselves so that the man receives the man's serve and the woman receives the woman's serve.

If C's return of serve gives A a chance to initiate an attack, and D's return of serve does not pose any threat to B, then align yourselves so that A handles C's return of serve.

If A hits strokes that are difficult for C to return, and B hits strokes difficult for D to return, A should receive D's serve, and B thus deals with C's shots.

Teamwork

The secret of winning doubles is to have full confidence in each other and coordinate your efforts so that you work together as one person. Do not claim credit for yourself. Encourage each other and try to set up opportunities for each other. Never blame a partner if he or she misses a shot.

PHYSICAL CONDITIONING

THE RISE IN TABLE TENNIS STANDARDS HAS BEEN AC-
companied by great demands on the players for speed,
quick reflexes and powerful strokes. Many young
players, after they have undergone the basic training
for table tennis, come to the realization that they lack
the physical ability and stamina to proceed with
more advanced training. Others later fail to reach
world-class status because they lack conditioning.
Thus it becomes absolutely necessary for young players to undertake a fitness training program in con-
junction with training in technique if they intend
to progress to higher levels of play in table tennis.

A general physical fitness program

Track, calisthenics and agility exercises will develop and strengthen muscles to enable a player to build up speed and endurance and improve flexibility, all conducive to more forceful strokes in table tennis. Tests show some world-class players are able to execute a stroke in 0.2 to 0.25 second. This places a high premium on judgment and reflexes. Modern techniques also call for great speed afoot. A player who can move around quickly and spontaneously will execute the strokes with confidence and eventually establish control of the table.

The driving force from the arm, body and wrist all contribute to the power of your strokes. In training, the player should learn how to position the feet to exert more power without loss of balance.

In the early stages of training, speed, reflexes and agility should be stressed. Later, emphasize strength and endurance.

Overall physical conditioning is the foundation of table tennis.

Special exercises to develop alertness, agility, fortitude and strength

At the same time as physical conditioning and strategic training are proceeding, special body-building exercises should be started for players learning the advanced strokes. You can practice with or without table tennis balls. The exercises should be tailored to individual needs, according to each player's style. For example, the aggressive attacker needs more practice in foot movements associated with attacking, and the defensive player needs to emphasize those foot movements associated with chopping and that style of play.

Pointers

Plan a program for each player according to sex, age and physical condition. Do not exercise too long or overextend your capabilities. Proceed gradually.

Before exercising, examine the equipment you will be using to make sure it's functional and safe. After exercising, store the equipment to safeguard against accidents.

You will build muscle strength in the arms if you practice with weight on your arm while hitting high balls.

Overall Physical Conditioning Exercises

SPEED

1. *Quick movement:*
   Run 30 meters, stop, rest and run again at different speed.
2. *Quick start:*
   a. Start running on signal.
   b. Relay running.
3. *Reflexes:*
   a. All kinds of running.
   b. Games.

4. Jumping, jogging, knee bends and short runs.
Repeat these exercises, which are designed to develop
thigh muscles, to strengthen the back, waist and knee
muscles, and to increase speed in foot movements and
control.

AGILITY

1. On signal, run forward or backward, right or left.
   Relay runs with obstacles.
2. Run fast and stop. Run fast, turn around and run
   fast again.
3. Jump quickly, first on one leg, then two legs.
4. Bend the body back and straighten, keeping body
   balance. Repeat several times.
5. Movements related to table tennis strokes.
Stress balance and agility in these exercises.

STRENGTH

1. Bend the body back and straighten. Repeat several
   times.
2. Do squat jumps with the hands on the legs.
3. High jumps and distance jumps.
4. Bend your elbows holding a small dumbbell.
5. Throw and catch a solid ball.

STAMINA

For speed and endurance:
1. Long-distance running, 800 to 3000 meters.

2. Short dashes, 20 to 30 meters.

3. Short dashes at different speeds.

4. Jump rope for 20 seconds.

The above exercises may be repeated as many times as necessary for individual needs.

For strength and endurance:

Repeat the exercises in the strength column five to ten times gradually.

FLEXIBILITY

Exercises for one person:

Shoulder turning exercises, sit-ups (keeping legs down on floor), kicking exercises, bending forward and backward, sideways, left and right, and waist twisting and pivoting.

Exercises for two persons:

a. Two persons sit back-to-back on the floor. Spread the legs apart and stretch. Interlock each other's arms tightly. One person keeps the head as low as possible and tries to turn the upper body.

b. One person lies face down on the floor, the other sits on his back and with both hands on the partner's chest tries to pull him up. The partner stretches the arms out to left and right and bends as far back as possible.

c. Two persons stand back-to-back with the arms interlocked. One bends forward to lift up partner. Do six to ten times. Bend a little more each time.

Special Exercises for Speed, Agility,
Strength and Stamina

SPEED AND AGILITY

1. *Tiptoe and jump rope:* To strengthen the calf muscles and the heel, tiptoe and jump as high as possible.
2. *Hand movement exercises:* Stress coordination, speed and accuracy.
3. *Foot movement exercises;*
   a. *For attackers:* Review the foot movement exercises for
      (1) Backhand push/forehand attack
      (2) Backhand attack combined with forehand attack (standing sideways)
      (3) Smash (standing sideways)
      You may do the above exercises two ways: either a fixed number of times, or by fixed time.
   b. *For defensive players:*
      Designate a certain area to practice forehand and backhand chops and short shots. Practice foot movements forward and backward at the same time.
   c. Designate an area of about 2.5 meters square to practice the two-step jump-over and the quick jump-over. Practice a certain number of each step in 30-second intervals.
4. *Combined exercises:*
   a. *Placement practice:* Divide the opponent's court into six areas with designated numbers. The

coach calls a number for the player each time, gradually increasing the speed of calling. Try to hit the designated area the coach calls.

b. *Shadow practice:* Shadow practice the basic strokes, stressing speed and accuracy.

c. *Two-person practice without balls:* Watch the opponent's racket movement to determine spins and placements.

d. *Concentrated ball practice:* Stress speed, change of spins and placements and reflexes to return an oncoming ball.

STRENGTH AND STAMINA

1. Increase speed and number of times on all the exercises listed under Speed and Agility.
2. Concentrated ball practice on how to kill a high ball with controlled placements to opponent's side, from near the net to the back.
3. Use a weighted racket (weighing not more than one kilo) to hit balls to strengthen arm muscles.
4. *For strengthening the wrist:*
   a. Hold the racket in your hand and practice wrist snaps or flicks.
   b. Hold a small dumbbell in your right hand. Support the right forearm with your left hand. Use your wrist to twirl the dumbbell. (Left-handers exercise with left hand.)
5. *For stamina:*
   Lengthen the time of practice.

HOW TO DEVELOP A TRAINING PROGRAM

PLANNING A TRAINING PROGRAM AND CARRYING IT out scientifically are of utmost importance. First, a training goal should be established. Then the stages of training to attain that goal should be worked out in detail. Many of our top-ranking players have, by following a well-planned program, achieved spectacular results in five or six years.

Here are guidelines to follow:

Establish a proper mental approach by following the ideology of the proletariat to eliminate class struggle and to serve the country.

Develop a training program, taking into account that

1. Physical fitness is just as important as training in technique.

2. Matches should be held periodically to stimulate competitive interest.
3. Overall training and specific training should be combined.
4. Special training for individual needs should be combined with regular training.

The director of the program should schedule group meetings with the players to discuss the goals of the program.

In setting up a program, the individual needs of each player should be considered. Plan a program to help the player improve progressively, at the same time encouraging the player to develop his or her individual strengths and style of play.

Young players should strive to finish the basic training in two years, doing three hours of physical exercises a day. Within five years, young players should not only know the strokes and tactics but also know how to control and use them effectively. Usually the last two or three years of training can be devoted to improving the player's own style of play.

Beginners should practice about two hours a day, or 10 to 12 hours a week. In advanced training, practice runs 3 to 3½ hours a day, or about 18 hours a week. Don't exercise on national holidays or festivals, but make up the lost time during summer and winter vacations.

Master one stroke before learning another.

Ratio of physical conditioning and technique training:

Beginner's level—physical conditioning 25% to 30%, technique training 70% to 75%

Advanced level—physical conditioning 20% to 25%, technical training 75% to 80%

Tactical level—physical conditioning 15% to 20%, technique training 80% to 85%

Apart from daily classes offering discussion and constructive criticism, monthly competitions should be held to measure development and promote interest. Each player's progress should be recorded. If a player does not show improvement, the coach should investigate.

CHAMPIONSHIP TOURNAMENTS

THE TOURNAMENT IS THE PROVING GROUND FOR THE training program. Competition gives young players a chance to learn new techniques and styles as well as to determine where other players made mistakes. "Friendship first, competition second" is the slogan for the Chinese table tennis team. At international tournaments, the Chinese players have followed the slogan faithfully and made friends around the world. They have demonstrated not only their courage and aggressiveness but also their eagerness to observe and learn new techniques.

TOURNAMENT PREPARATIONS

Develop the right mental approach. Many inexperienced players tend to get so tense before a tournament they cannot eat or sleep. They become too excited to concentrate and too nervous to care whether they win or lose. These aberrations arise from an unsound mental approach. The leader or coach should help the players to overcome these tensions early in training. Young players should understand the goal of competition is not personal glory but honoring one's country.

Conserve physical strength and stamina. Tournaments run a long time. Especially near the end, opponents become tougher and the competition keener. Stamina plays an important part in determining the champion. So before a tournament (1) shorten practice time, (2) avoid strenuous exercise, (3) arrange rest periods, (4) eat properly.

Study your opponents to determine their strong and weak points, the strategies they are likely to use, the extent of their stamina and any other useful information. Analyze the findings with a coach to formulate a strategy that offers the most promising avenues to exploit.

The leader and coaches should make decisions together and give clear instructions to the players so there is no misunderstanding.

Inspect your equipment to make sure it is functional. (Don't forget to take your equipment with you.)

Confirm the time and place you are scheduled to play.

TOURNAMENT POINTERS

Affirm the conclusions made in advance about your opposition and be prepared to revise your strategy if it's not effective.

Have confidence to win and courage to fight aggressively for control of the table, also the determination to defend when under attack and to counterattack to regain the initiative. Don't lose confidence if you should make errors.

Don't become lax if you are winning or discouraged if you are losing. Maintain your poise under attack. On defense, plan to counterattack as swiftly as possible. Don't be timid about implementing your tactics.

Show faith in the coach and obey instructions. Make sure you understand them fully. At the same time, don't rely entirely on the coach. Make your own judgments, too. In the cauldron of competition, there often is no time to seek counsel.

POINTERS FOR COACHES

Be specific in your instructions.

Oversee the strategy cool-headedly. Be calm. Don't lose your temper or become pessimistic.

Compare the quality of your players with the opposition and devise a draw that gives you the most advantageous pairings. Remember, often the stamina of a player is just as important as tactical ability.

Keep records of the tournament results for later use. From the record, you can plan your training program more insightfully. After each match analyze the factors that influenced the outcome. After the tournament, review the results with each player.

TOURNAMENT STRUCTURE

Generally, table tennis tournaments fall into two basic categories: (1) team competition, (2) singles and doubles competition. The team competition is divided into men's and women's championships. The singles and doubles competition breaks down into men's and women's singles, men's and women's doubles, and mixed doubles.

In singles, the winner is the first player to win three games. The most common format is the round robin, where players are gradually eliminated until the two best players confront each other for the title.

In men's team competition, each team is composed of three players. In turn, the players play a total of nine games. The team that takes five games wins.

Order of Appearance of Each Player in Men's Team Competition
(*Host team players designated* **A**, **B**, **C**; *visiting team players* **X**, **Y**, **Z**.)

	First Match*		Second Match		Third Match	
	Team	Player	Team	Player	Team	Player
	Host	A	Host	B	Host	C
	Guest	X	Guest	Y	Guest	Z
Game No.	1 5 9		2 4 7		3 6 8	
	1 4 8		2 6 9		3 5 7	

* The first match is played by **A** and **X** in the first game.
In Game No. 5, player **A** plays player **Z**.
In Game No. 9, player **A** plays player **Y**.

As we can see from the above chart, each player of the host team plays a different player from the visiting team each time.

A Record of Men's Team Competition

Group No.	Date	Time	Table No.

_____ Team

vs.

_____ Team

Game No.	Name of host team		Player No.	Name of guest team		Player No.	Game Scores			Final score
	Players A, B, C.			Players X, Y, Z.			#1	#2	#3	
	Des. No.	Name		Des. No.	Name					
1										
2										
3										
4										
5										
6										
7										
8										
9										

Final score _____

Name of captain of winning team _____

Name of referees _____

Name of winning team _____

Name of captain of losing team _____

In the women's team competition, each team consists of two to four players. The first two games are singles. The third game is doubles, in which any two players from each team can play. The fourth and fifth games are singles. The team that takes three games wins.

Order of Appearance of Each Player (*Women's Team Competition*)
(*Host team players designated A and B, guest team players, X and Y*)

Game No.	First Match Host team player A Guest team player X		Second Match Host team player B Guest team player Y		Third Match Either A, B, X, Y or others
	1	4	2	5	Doubles
	1	5	2	4	Doubles

A Record of Women's Team Competition

Group No.	Date	Time	Table No.

_____ Team

vs. _____ Team

Game No.	Name of host team		Player No.	Name of guest team		Player No.	Game scores			Final score
	Players A and B			Players X and Y			#1	#2	#3	
	Des. No.	Name		Des. No.	Name					
1										
2										
3										
4										
5										

Final score _____

Name of winning team _____

Name of captain of winning team _____

Name of captain of losing team _____

Name of referees _____

TEAM LINEUPS

In the team competition, the selection of the players and the order of appearance—matching the players against the opposition advantageously—are of extreme importance. Before compiling the lineup, the coach should correlate all of the information available on both teams.

Following are some of the most conventional methods of devising a lineup:

Men's host team

First match (player A): This player should have experience and determination. Stamina is a less important consideration because the player does not have to play again until Game No. 5 and will have ample opportunity to recover any loss of strength.

Second match (player B): This should be the best player.

Third match (player C): This should be an older player who may not have strong technique but instead offers extensive experience.

Men's guest team

First match (player X): This player will likely play the second-best player on the host team. Some coaches like to put their best player in the first match but most use their most experienced here.

Second match (player Y): This player need not have great physical stamina.

Third match (player Z): The best player normally plays here. The premium is on physical stamina.

Matching players for women's team competition

Because there are fewer games in women's team competition, matching the players is usually simpler. The most important game is generally the fourth game, which is played by player A of the host team against player Y of the visiting team.

APPENDIX

Statistics Chart Showing Attack Techniques Used in Table Tennis Competition

Name of player _____ Type _____ Name of opponent _____ Type _____ Date _____

Description		Game No. 1	Game No. 2	Game No. 3	Game No. 4	Game No. 5	Scores Win	Lose	% of Win
Service and attack	Serve								
	Attack								
	Spin								
Return of service	Receive								
	Attack								
	Spin								
	Under attack								
Short chop	Short chop								
	Attack								
	Spin								
Exchange of attack shots	Forehand								
	Sideways								
	Backhand								
Loopspin	Forehand								
	Sideways								

Under attack	Forehand								
	Backhand								
	Under attack								
Return of loopspins	Forehand								
	Push								
Push-block	Exchange of								
	Push-blocks								
	Placement								
Spins followed with surprise attack									
Killing a chance shot									
Short shot									
Other									
Comparison of scores									
Mental alertness and behavior									
Use of strategy									
Result of competition									

Winning team ——————

Statistician ——————

Statistics Chart Showing Defense Techniques Used in Table Tennis Competition

Name of player _____   Type _____   Name of opponent _____   Type _____   Date _____

Description		Game No. 1	Game No. 2	Game No. 3	Game No. 4	Game No. 5	Scores Win	Scores Lose	Scores % of Win
Return of service									
Short chops	Forehand								
	Backhand								
Chops	Forehand								
	Backhand								
Return of surprise attack shots	Forehand								
	Middle								
	Backhand								
Return of short shots									
Return of loops									
Service and attack	Service								
	Attack								
	Spin								
Short chop	Forehand								

Chops and counterattack	Forehand							
	Backhand							
Block								
Loopspin								
Loopspin and surprise attack								
Continuous attack shots								
Lobbing								
Unexpected shots								
Comparison of scores								
Mental alertness and behavior								
Use of strategy								

Result of competition _____ Winning team _____

Statistician _____